S0-BRL-553

OXFORD READINGS IN PHILOSOPHY

Series Editor G. J. Warnock

THE PHILOSOPHY OF LANGUAGE

THE PHILOSOPHY
OF LANGUAGE

Edited by

J. R. SEARLE

OXFORD UNIVERSITY PRESS

1971

Oxford University Press, Ely House, London W.1

GLASGOW   NEW YORK   TORONTO   MELBOURNE   WELLINGTON
CAPE TOWN   SALISBURY   IBADAN   NAIROBI   DAR ES SALAAM   LUSAKA   ADDIS ABABA
BOMBAY   CALCUTTA   MADRAS   KARACHI   LAHORE   DACCA
KUALA LUMPUR   SINGAPORE   HONG KONG   TOKYO

FILMSET AND PRINTED IN GREAT BRITAIN
BY BUTLER & TANNER LTD., FROME AND LONDON

CONTENTS

INTRODUCTION

It is important to distinguish between the philosophy of language and linguistic philosophy. Linguistic philosophy consists in the attempt to solve philosophical problems by analysing the meanings of words, and by analysing logical relations between words in natural languages. This may be done in order to solve such traditional philosophical problems as those concerning determinism, scepticism, and causation; or it may be done without special regard to *traditional* problems but as an investigation of concepts for their own interest, as an inquiry into certain aspects of the world by scrutinizing the classifications and distinctions we make in the language we use to characterize or describe the world. The philosophy of language consists in the attempt to analyse certain general features of language such as meaning, reference, truth, verification, speech acts, and logical necessity.

'The philosophy of language' is the name of a subject matter within philosophy; 'linguistic philosophy' is primarily the name of a philosophical method. But the two, method and subject, are intimately connected. Both because some of the problems in the philosophy of language can be profitably attacked by the methods of linguistic philosophy (the problems concerning the nature of truth, for example, may be regarded, at least in part, as questions about the analysis of the concept 'true') and, more importantly, because the methods linguistic philosophers employ in conducting linguistic analyses depend crucially on their philosophy of language. The way a linguistic philosopher conducts an actual investigation will depend on certain general conceptions he has concerning how words mean and how they relate to the world. It is only given some general theory of or approach to language that one can even get started on a particular linguistic analysis. It is for this reason—among others—that in the spread of analytical philosophy in the twentieth century the philosophy of language has occupied such a central, some would say *the* central, place in the entire enterprise of philosophy. Most of the influential philosophers of this century, for example, Russell, Wittgenstein, Carnap, Quine, Austin, and Strawson, have been in varying degrees philosophers of language.

Though both the philosophy of language and linguistic philosophy are pursued nowadays with more self-consciousness than ever before, both are in fact as old as philosophy. When in the *Euthyphro* Plato asks what is piety, he may be regarded as asking a question concerning the concept *pious,* and this, most contemporary philosophers would claim, may be regarded as a question concerning the exact meaning of the Greek word for pious, 'hosion', and its synonyms in other languages. When in the *Phaedo* he advances the theory that general terms get their meaning by standing for the Forms he is advancing a thesis in the philosophy of language, a thesis about how words mean.

In spite of a historical continuity stretching back to the Greeks, there are good reasons for dating the beginnings of modern philosophy of language in the work of the German philosopher and mathematician, Gottlob Frege. Frege wanted to show that mathematics was reducible to and founded on logic. To carry out this enterprise he had to invent a new logical system. In the course of his logical investigations he found the prevailing nineteenth-century views about language—represented most influentially by J. S. Mill—to be rather superficial and in many cases downright false, so he was forced to develop a theory of his own.

In order to place contemporary work in the philosophy of language in some historical perspective, and to give the reader a general idea of the background to the essays in this volume, I shall now—all too briefly—sketch some of the more important developments in the philosophy of language, beginning with Frege. What I say will be nothing more than a rough outline, and the reader should not consider the simplicity of the account as reflecting any simplicity in the actual development of this subject.

Frege's most important single discovery in the philosophy of language was the distinction between sense and reference. He elucidated this distinction in terms of the following puzzle about identity statements: How is it possible for a true statement of the form, *a is identical with b*, to contain any more factual information than a statement of the form, *a is identical with a*?[1] If we construe the statements as being about the objects referred to by the names which replace 'a' and 'b', it seems that they must say exactly the same uninformative thing, namely, that an object is identical with itself. If, on the other hand, we construe identity statements as about the names used in making them then it seems they must be arbitrary, since we can arbitrarily assign any name to any object we like. Yet obviously the statement 'The Evening Star is the Morning Star' does not mean the same as, and is more factually informative than, the statement 'The Evening Star is the Evening Star'. How is this possible? Frege's answer is that in addition to the name and the object it refers to, viz. its *reference*, there is a third element, its *sense* (or as we might prefer to say in English: the meaning or descriptive content) of the name in virtue of which and only in virtue of which it refers to its reference. The sense provides the 'mode of presentation' of the object, and referring to a reference is always achieved by way of sense. The reason why 'The Evening Star is the Morning Star' can be more factually informative than 'The Evening Star is the Evening Star', even though the reference is the same, is that the sense of 'The Evening Star' is different from the sense of 'The Morning Star', and the statement conveys that one and the same object has the features specified in the different senses of the two expressions. Frege regards this theory of sense and refer-

[1] Frege, G., 'Sense and Reference', *Philosophical Writings*, trans. P. T. Geach and M. Black (Blackwell, Oxford, 1952).

ence as applying not only to definite descriptions like 'the man in a blue shirt' but also to ordinary proper names like 'Chicago' and 'Winston Churchill'.

Frege then extends this distinction from singular referring expressions to predicate expressions and to whole sentences. He says that in addition to expressing their sense, predicate expressions refer to concepts, and he says of sentences (at least those where the question of truth or falsity arises) that they express a *thought* as their sense, and have a *truth value* (i.e. the circumstance that they are true or the circumstance that they are false) as their reference. This extension of the distinction between sense and reference to predicates and whole sentences is less compelling and has been historically less influential than the original distinction for referring expressions. To my mind it loses the most brilliant insight of the original distinction, an insight which reveals the connection between reference and truth: namely that an expression refers to an object only because it conveys something true of that object. But a predicate does not convey something true of a concept nor does a sentence convey something true of a truth value. But one important feature of Frege's account of sentences has survived. Frege says that we must distinguish between the thought expressed by a sentence and the assertion of that thought. Thus, for example, the same thought is expressed by the sentence 'Socrates is wise' and 'Is Socrates wise?', and again, this same thought is expressed in the antecedent clause of 'If Socrates is wise then he is a philosopher'. But only in the first of these three sentences is that thought asserted. This distinction between the thought or content (or as most philosophers nowadays call it, the *proposition*) and the *assertion* of that proposition is important for the arguments in my article and in Grice's article in this volume.

After Frege the next great work in the philosophy of language was done by Russell in the years before the First World War and carried on by his student Wittgenstein in the *Tractatus Logico-Philosophicus*. Both Russell and Wittgenstein, for different sets of reasons, rejected the distinction between sense and reference. They thought that it might appear to work for simple cases, but that under a really rigorous analysis of language into its most elementary forms the relation between words and the world would turn out to be different from Frege's account of it. I regard the rejection of the theory of sense and reference by these two as a major mistake, and the reasons they give for rejecting it seem to me bad reasons.[2] However, having rejected it they developed a theory of how words relate to the world which was quite different from Frege's.

Russell[3] begins by considering a problem posed by sentences which contain definite descriptions with no corresponding object, for example, 'The King of France is bald.' This is obviously a meaningful sentence, but the puzzle is: how can it be meaningful since there is no King of France, hence there is nothing for the proposition

[2] See J. R. Searle, 'Russell's Rejection of Frege's Theory of Sense and Reference', *Analysis,* 1958, for a critical examination of Russell's reasons.

[3] 'On Denoting', *Mind* (1905).

expressed by the sentence to be about, hence there is nothing for the predicate to be either true or false of? How can a sentence be meaningful, if apparently the proposition it expresses is neither true nor false? Frege's answer was that a sentence could have sense even though the subject expression had no reference. The sentence might lack a truth value but the lack of a truth value does not render the sentence meaningless. To suppose mistakenly that it does is simply to confuse sense and reference. But Russell, having already rejected Frege's theory of sense and reference, gave the following different answer: the sentence appears to be of subject-predicate form but is not really so. Its grammatical form is misleading as to its logical form, and its logical form is that of a conjunction of statements—one of which is an existential statement. Under analysis the sentence really says:

> There is a King of France.
> There is not more than one King of France.
> Whatever is King of France is bald.

In this interpretation we are able to see that the original sentence is meaningful, and the proposition expressed by it is false. The proposition is false since there is no King of France.

It is important to see the difference between Frege and Russell here. Frege asks: how do proper names and definite descriptions refer to things? His answer is: in virtue of their sense. Russell rejects the question. He argues, in effect, that neither definite descriptions nor ordinary proper names (since ordinary proper names are just disguised or abbreviated definite descriptions for him) refer at all. Rather, he says, they have no meaning 'in isolation', but sentences containing them are to be analysed on the model of the analysis of sentences containing the expression 'The King of France', an analysis in which they no longer occur in their original form at all. All that is left are predicates, logical constants, and expressions such as 'there is a', 'something', 'nothing', 'anything', 'whatever', etc., none of which refer to particular objects.

But how do words hook on the the world for Russell, if definite description and ordinary proper names do not *refer*? Part of his answer is that there is a class of expressions of unanalysable simplicity, which are the *logically* proper names. They simply stand for entities without having any sense or meaning other than standing for entities. This conception is most fully worked out by Wittgenstein in the *Tractatus*.

In the *Tractatus* the point of contact between words and the world is provided by names. 'The name means the object. The object is its meaning.'[4] An elementary sentence of a language is simply an arrangement or concatenation of names, and since all meaningful sentences of a language are, for Wittgenstein, ultimately analysable into truth functional combinations of the elementary sentences, these names play the crucial role of relating words to things in the world. But if, as Wittgenstein says, elementary sentences are arrangements of names, how does a sentence come to have

[4] *Tractatus*, 3.203.

a sense? How does it differ from, for example, a list of names? Wittgenstein's answer is that the arrangement of names in the sentence constitutes a picture of a fact. Different ways of arranging names in sentences make the sentences different pictures of facts, and the sense of a sentence is provided by this picturing relationship. If there actually is a fact such as the picture represents, the sentence will be true; if not, the sentence will be false. The picturing relationship may be completely conventional. Thus in order to say that x is on top of y, one does not have to place the letter 'x' on top of the letter 'y'; one can, by convention, write 'x' followed by 'is on top of' followed by 'y'. Here, 'is on top of' is not another name but is part of a conventional way of picturing the relationship between x and y when x is on top of y. The fact that words are arranged in a sentence in a certain way pictures the fact that things are arranged in the world in a certain way.

This version of the picture theory of meaning encounters enormous difficulties, and in Wittgenstein's later work, the *Philosophical Investigations,* he rejects it completely. One difficulty is this: if the meaning of a name is literally the object for which it stands, then it seems the existence of these objects cannot be a matter of ordinary contingent fact. The reason for this is that the destruction of any contingently existing object such as a mountain or a car cannot destroy the meaning of any words, because any change in contingent features of the world must still be describable in words. Indeed, it seems it would make no sense to assert or deny the existence of the objects named by names. As Wittgenstein says, 'Objects make up the substance of the world' and 'Substance is what exists independently of what is the case'.[5] Unfortunately he never gives us any examples of objects or names or elementary sentences but says that sentences of ordinary language must be analysable into elementary sentences if they are to be fully meaningful. Paradoxically though—and this is a disadvantage from which Frege's philosophy of language did not suffer—ordinary names like 'Winston Churchill' and 'San Francisco' are not on his account 'names', and ordinary objects are not 'objects' in his sense.

One of the aims of the *Tractatus* was to delimit the realm of meaningful from meaningless discourse. In spite of its obscurity it exerted a profound influence in the 1920s and 30s, especially on *the logical positivists*, a group of empirically oriented philosophers interested in science and mathematics. They developed, partly from the *Tractatus* and partly from other remarks of Wittgenstein, a criterion of meaningfulness, the Verification Principle. This principle states that the meaning of a proposition is its method of verification, or put less obscurely: all meaningful statements are either analytic on the one hand or empirical and synthetic on the other. All analytic truths are true be definition, whereas all true empirical statements are true in virtue of the sense experiences which verify them; indeed, they are equivalent in meaning to the sets of basic propositions recording sense experiences which would constitute their verification.

[5] *Tractatus* 2.021, 2.024.

Among the many objections made to the Verification Theory of Meaning is this: What is the status of the Verification Principle itself? Surely the principle is not synthetic, for it cannot be just a contingent empirical trait of meaningful utterances that they are verifiable. But if the principle is analytic, is it not just an arbitrary definition of meaningfulness, which one may or may not choose to accept? And, indeed, it appears to be quite inconsistent with our ordinary definitions of 'meaningful' and 'meaningless'. Or is the verification principle itself meaningless, like the metaphysics it was intended to destroy? These difficulties, along with that of finding a version of the Verification Principle that could be precisely stated, continued to plague the positivists in the years before the Second World War.

Notice that all these theories which I have sketched—Frege, the *Tractatus*, logical positivism—have certain characteristics in common. They all assume that the only, at any rate the primary, aim of language is to represent and communicate factual information, that the part of language that really counts is the 'cognitive' part. The aim of language, in short, is to communicate what can be true or false. Secondly, they treat the elements of language—words, sentences, propositions—as things that represent or things that are true or false, etc., apart from any actions or intentions of speakers and hearers. The elements of the language, not the actions and intentions of the speakers are what count. In the late thirties and especially after the Second World War these assumptions came to be vigorously challenged, especially by Wittgenstein. Wittgenstein argued that stating facts is only one of the countless jobs we do with language and that the meaning of elements lies not in any relationship they have in the abstract but in the use we make of them. 'Language', says Wittgenstein, 'is an instrument';[6] and 'for a large class of cases, . . . the meaning of a word is its use in the language'.[7]

Austin, in a similar vein, called attention to a class of utterances that do not even set out to be true or false. For example, a man who says, 'I promise I will come', is not stating a fact about himself to the effect that he promises, but rather he is *making* a promise. Austin called such utterances 'performatives', contrasting them with 'constatives'.

There was a good deal of carelessness in the way philosophers in this period talked about the *use* of expressions and—with the notable exception of Austin—they did not always distinguish among the different sorts of 'use' to which expressions could be put. But this approach has certain real advantages which have survived to the present day and which influence several of the articles in this volume. Most importantly it recasts the discussion of many problems in the philosophy of language into the larger context of the discussion of human action and behaviour generally. Questions of meaning and reference can be seen in the context of speakers meaning something by something and referring to something in the utterance of an expression.

[6] *Philosophical Investigations*, para. 569.
[7] Op. cit., para. 43.

Instead of seeing the relations between words and the world as something existing *in vacuo*, one now sees them as involving intentional actions by speakers, employing conventional devices (words, sentences) in accordance with extremely abstract sets of rules for the use of those devices. For example, the real strength of Frege's theory of sense and reference as opposed to Russell's theory of definite descriptions emerges in Strawson's conception of reference as a speech act.[8] Once one sees referring as an action that is performed in the utterance of an expression with a particular sense provided by the rules for the use of the expression, then it is easier to see that it is subject to the sorts of error that plague actions generally (one can fail to refer to a king of France for the same reason that one can fail to hit a king of France: there is no such person), and on this account there is much less motivation for trying to identify referring (one kind of speech act), with asserting an existential proposition (quite another kind of speech act), as Russell in effect does.

Which brings us to the articles in this volume. Austin once expressed the belief that the work being done by philosophers, grammarians, psychologists, linguists, etc., in this century would eventually result in a science of language in much the same way that nineteenth- and early twentieth-century work in logic by people of various disciplines 'resulted in a science of logic. We have by no means yet achieved that result, but the articles in this volume, I hope, will indicate something of the direction from which I think it may come. They divide roughly into two sections. The first four articles centre around the notion of speech acts and the relation of meaning to speech acts; the rest deal with the implications of generative grammar.

In the first four articles we proceed historically from Austin's attempts to revise the performative-constative distinction to current research on speech acts. Austin in 'Performative-Constative' attacks the very distinction he originally made famous, that between performative and constative utterances. But he attacks it from an interesting angle. The original distinction was supposed to be a distinction between utterances which are *sayings* (statements, descriptions, etc.) and utterances which are *doings* of some other kinds (e.g. promises, bets, warnings). It is supposed to be a distinction between utterances which are not acts (constatives), and utterances which are acts (performatives). But, as Austin argues in this article and his posthumously published lectures, *How To Do Things with Words*, constatives turn out to be speech acts as well. Making a statement or giving a description is as much performing a speech act as making a promise or giving an order. So what were originally presented as special cases of utterances (performatives) now are seen to swallow the general cases (constatives), which turn out to be only one class of speech acts among others. Austin, in his subsequent terminology, calls these different kinds of complete speech acts (statements, bets, warnings, promises, etc.) *illocutionary* acts, and contrasts them with acts which involve achieving certain effects on hearers such as persuading,

---

[8] Strawson, P. F., 'On Referring', *Mind,* 1950, reprinted A. Flew (ed.), *Essays in Conceptual Analysis* (Macmillan, London, 1956).

convincing, frightening, boring, amusing, annoying, which he calls *perlocutionary* acts.

Both Strawson and I, in quite different ways and with differing objectives, attempt to interpret Austin's account of the notion of an illocutionary act in terms of Grice's analysis of *meaning*. Grice analyses meaning as intending to produce an effect in a hearer by getting him to recognize the intention to produce that effect.[9] Strawson probes the extent to which illocutionary acts are matters of *convention* and *intention* respectively in light of Austin's claim that illocutionary acts are essentially conventional. He concludes that some acts are indeed essentially conventional in that they require *extra-linguistic* conventions for their performance. For example a marriage ceremony, calling someone 'out' in a game, bidding at bridge, etc., are all essentially conventional in that they require some extra-linguistic conventions for their performances; but the great bulk of fundamental types of illocutionary acts, statements, questions, requests, etc., for Strawson are not conventional in that or any other than the trivial sense that they can be performed with conventional devices and they have conventional names. The contrast between the two types of cases emerges when we see that the non-conventional acts will be successfully performed if the 'complex overt intention' of the speaker is grasped by the hearer, that is if he *understands*. But the overt intended effect of the speech act may still not be achieved without any breach of rules or conventions. With the conventional act, on the other hand, any failure of the speaker to achieve his overt intention must be attributable to some breach of rule or convention. In the one case therefore (the conventional case) the explicit performative form may be the name of the very act which is performed if and only if the speaker's overt intention is effective; but in the other case (the non-conventional case) it cannot be the name of this act.

I think this distinction does not have the force that Strawson attributes to it, and that it, as well as Grice's original account of meaning, suffers from a failure to appreciate adequately Austin's distinction between illocutionary uptake (i.e. understanding the utterance) and perlocutionary effect. Strawson and Grice both think of the 'overt intention' of the speaker in the non-conventional case as the eliciting of some response or effect in the hearer, such as, e.g., getting him to believe something (the overt intended effect of statements) or getting him to do something (the overt intended effect of requests). But, I wish to claim, the intended effect of meaning something is that the hearer should know the illocutionary force and propositional content of the utterance, not that he should respond or behave in such and such ways. I hint at this point in my article in this volume, and I argue for it more fully in *Speech Acts*.[10] Here, for the sake of brevity, I state it rather dogmatically.

---

[9] Grice, H. P., 'Meaning', *Philosophical Review,* 1957, reprinted P. F. Strawson (ed.), *Philosophical Logic* (Oxford University Press, London, 1967).

[10] Searle, J. R., *Speech Acts, An Essay in the Philosophy of Language* (Cambridge University Press, London and New York, 1969), pp. 42–50.

Once that point is seen, then the difference Strawson cites does not appear so great. Compare making a statement (non-conventional) and bidding at bridge (conventional). In both cases the intended effect of meaning something is that the hearer should understand the utterance. In the bidding case this is facilitated by some linguistic conventions to the effect that certain bids are to be made under certain conditions. In both cases the intended *perlocutionary* effect may not be achieved, e.g. the hearer may not believe my statement, or he may not believe I have as many high cards as my five no-trump bid would indicate. And in neither case does he breach any rules or conventions if he fails to believe me. Furthermore, even in those cases where failure to secure the perlocutionary effect does indeed involve a breach of rules, this is only for the trivial reason that the rules are designed to enforce the perlocutionary effect. For example, if I fail to perform my duties under a contract I do indeed destroy the intended perlocutionary effect of the contract and thus violate the law. But this coincidence involves no deep linguistic point, it merely illustrates that the law in this case is designed to ensure the *perlocutionary* effect once the *illocutionary* performance has been satisfactorily done.

In both the statement case and the contract case the performative verb is the name of the act which is performed if the overt intention is effective, because in the one case the overt intention is to make a statement and in the other it is to make a contract. To suppose otherwise is to suppose what I am alleging is a mistake, namely that the overt intentions of meaning something are perlocutionary.

Furthermore—and this is a quite separate point—the question of to what extent the 'nonconventional acts' of statement making, etc., are conventional is not conclusively settled. For both Grice and Strawson the basic speech acts are not essentially conventional at all. They believe that it just so happens that we do have linguistic conventions for achieving what are natural responses like beliefs and actions. The picture presented in my article is that for some acts at least, e.g. statements and promises, the acts can only be performed within systems of 'constitutive' rules and the particular linguistic conventions we have in particular natural languages are simply conventional realizations of these underlying constitutive rules. This is one of the most important unresolved controversies in contemporary philosophy of language. It might be rephrased as follows: to what extent can such basic illocutionary notions as statement, request, promise, etc., be explicated without employing such notions as rule or convention, but employing only such notions as intention, response, procedure, etc.? The most promising work in the latter category is in Grice's William James lectures, a portion of which is published in this volume. In this article he attempts to analyse certain fundamental features of language using only 'brute' notions. My article attempts to explore the assumption that some types of illocutionary acts are necessarily conventional, i.e. can only be performed given certain constitutive rules. It is an assumption that I have by no means proven and which Grice may in the end succeed in disproving.

In Grice's article he continues work on the project, undertaken in his 1957 article, of explaining what it is for a sentence to mean something, and what it is for a word or phrase to mean something in terms of what it is for speakers to mean something by doing something. The basic notion, as in the earlier article, is the notion of a speaker performing an action and meaning something by that performance. Here Grice modifies his earlier definition of *meaning* in a way that partially, but not entirely, avoids the objections I just made. He characterizes the intended effect of imperative type utterances as being that the hearer should intend to do something rather than that he should actually do it; and he characterizes the intended effect of indicative type utterances as being, not that the hearer should believe something, but that he should believe that the speaker believes something. But this characterization still seems to me inadequate, for several reasons, of which here are two. First, it seems to me that a speaker may utter sentences, mean what he utters and still not have these intentions. For example, I may utter 'It's raining', mean *it's raining* by that utterance, and still not care a hang whether my hearer believes that I believe it's raining. The intended effect on the hearer of meaning it's raining when I say 'It's raining' and mean it (as opposed to just uttering 'It's raining' as a pronunciation practice, say) is that the hearer should know that he has been told (i.e. the statement has been made to him) that it is raining. The intended effect of meaning, in short, is understanding, which is an illocutionary not a perlocutionary effect.

Secondly, is is not clear how these definitions of meaning would discriminate among the many different kinds of illocutionary acts. For example, how on these definitions do we tell the difference between 'I'll do it', meant as a promise, and meant as a statement of intention? Both according to Grice involve the intention to produce in the hearer the belief that the speaker believes he will do the act, but this is not adequate to distinguish the two different *meant* illocutionary forces.

The last three sections are concerned with transformational generative grammar and its importance for philosophy. Such grammars are called 'generative' because they contain systems of rules for generating an infinite set of sentences and thus attempt to account for the ability of speakers of natural languages to produce and understand an indefinite number of completely new utterances, utterances of sentences they have never heard before. They are called transformational, because they contain transformational as well as phrase-structure rules. That is, they contain rules which transform the structure of sentences by rearranging or deleting elements as well as rules which structure sentences into such phrases as the noun phrase and the verb phrase. Indeed, one of the early achievements of this type of linguistic theory was its demonstration of the inadequacy of phrase-structure rules alone to account for the syntactical complexity of natural human languages.

Chomsky's work, of which I am attempting to provide philosophical readers a glimpse with the selections included in this volume, does not lend itself to the kind of piecemeal philosophical sniping that I have been making at the other authors because of its global and systematic character. It is important, however, to emphasize that from a philosopher's point of view a great deal is assumed and a great deal is left unclear. For example, Chomsky tells us as one of his 'uncontroversial' assumptions that 'the competence of the speaker-hearer can ideally be expressed as a system of rules that relate signals to semantic interpretations of those signals'. But that mastering competence in a language is a matter of mastering a system of rules as opposed to, say, acquiring a set of dispositions to behave, is a controversial—or at any rate challengeable—assumption. It happens to be a view I hold, but it is not an obvious truth. Furthermore, when Chomsky tells us that the child who learns the language acquires an 'internal representation' of these rules, it is not totally clear what such an internal representation is supposed to be. Is it supposed to mean that he has 'tacit knowledge' of the rules in the sense of Polanyi?[11] I rather think so. But the notion of an internal representation would, as far as Chomsky tells us, allow us to interpret it in other ways, e.g. as implying only that the idealized linguistic competence of the speaker-hearer can be described by these rules in the same way that the laws of physics describe the idealized behaviour of a falling body. In neither case, on such an interpretation, would we have to interpret the body or the speaker as *knowing* any rules.

Katz applies the semantic component of generative grammar in an attempt to solve certain traditional problems in the philosophy of language. It is not always clear that he solves as much as he claims to solve. For example, it is puzzling that he should think his explication of the notion of analyticity in terms of the concepts of semantic theory is an answer to Quine's doubts about analyticity, because Quine objects to any account that relies on notions such as meaning or semantic rules. But Katz's apparatus of semantic markers, projection rules, etc., is just as meaning-laden as Carnap's notion of a semantic rule, which Quine was originally concerned to attack. Katz presupposes intensional notions and does not explicate them in the extensional and behavioural fashion that Quine would regard as acceptable.

Again Katz's remarks about logical form settle none of the outstanding issues about logical form. The most serious contemporary philosophical dispute about logical form concerns Russell's theory of descriptions. Russell, as we have seen, maintains that sentences with a definite description as a grammatical subject are misleading as to their logical form. Grammatically, says Russell, they are of subject-predicate form, but their logical form is that of an existential sentence, not a subject-predicate sentence at all. It is hard to see how a Katzian interpretation of this issue would contribute anything at all to settling it except perhaps by begging the question in favour of Strawson, since there is nothing in the underlying phrase marker of, say, 'The King of France is bald' to show the Russellian distinction between existential and subject-predicate sentences.

The last section, a symposium between Chomsky, Putnam, and Goodman, concerns the innateness hypothesis. Chomsky and his followers claim that information

[11] Cf., e.g., Polanyi, M., *Personal Knowledge* (University of Chicago Press, 1960).

currently available in empirical linguistic theory supports the traditional rationalist conception of innate ideas, the theory that human beings have concepts implanted in their minds prior to any experiences. The dispute over this claim breaks down into two questions. First, a historical question: what did the rationalists mean by their doctrine of innate ideas and is it what Chomsky thinks they meant? And second, for our purposes the more interesting question: what assumptions must we make about the innate intellectual capacities of children to account for the way in which they acquire languages? In this symposium at least it is my opinion that Chomsky definitely has the better of the argument on the second question. Putnam and Goodman offer arguments to counter some of the claims made by the innateness theorists, but they do not come to grips with the more important of Chomsky's arguments. For example Chomsky claims that the rules relating deep and surface sentence structures are so complex and so abstract as to defy any stimulus-response or associationist account of their learning. Only by supposing that the child has the form of the grammar programmed into his brain can we account for his intellectual feat in acquiring these rules. This, at least in part, is an empirical issue: how complex and abstract are the syntactical rules of natural languages? In order to answer his claims, Chomsky's critics would have to show either that he is mistaken in his empirical theory of the syntax of natural languages or that he has drawn the wrong conclusion from that theory.

There are three main contemporary approaches to the philosophy of language: the neo-positivist–symbolic logic approach represented most ably by Quine, the so-called 'ordinary language' approach of Wittgenstein and Austin, and the generative grammar approach of Chomsky and his followers. I think, as the selections in this volume indicate, that the future development of the subject is likely to come from joining the two latter approaches.

I

PERFORMATIVE-CONSTATIVE

J. L. AUSTIN

Translator's Note: 'Performative-Constative' is a straightforward translation of Austin's paper 'Performatif-Constatif', which he wrote in French and presented at a (predominantly) Anglo-French conference held at Royaumont in March 1958. The case of the discussion which follows it[1] is somewhat more complex. The actual discussion at Royaumont was carried on in both French and English. What appears in the published volume after Austin's text (*Cahiers de Royaumont, Philosophie* No. IV, *La Philosophie Analytique:* Les Éditions de Minuit, 1962, pp. 271–304) is a version of this, based on a transcript but substantially cut and edited, in which the contributions originally made in English were translated into French by M. Béra. It might have been possible, for the present publication, to procure copies at least of those portions of the original transcript that were in English. However, it seemed to me preferable simply to translate into English the entire French text, mainly for the reason that it is this edited version, and this only, that all those taking part are known to have seen and approved for publication.

G. J. Warnock

One can quite easily get the idea of the performative utterance—though the expression, as I am well aware, does not exist in the French language, or anywhere else. This idea was brought in to mark a contrast with that of the declarative utterance, or rather, as I am going to call it, the constative utterance. And there we have straight off what I want to call in question. Ought we to accept this Performative-Constative antithesis?

The constative utterance, under the name, so dear to philosophers, of *statement*,[2] has the property of being true or false. The performance utterance, by contrast, can never be either: it has its own special job, it is used to perform an action. To issue such an utterance[3] *is* to perform the action—an action, perhaps, which one scarcely could perform, at least with so much precision, in any other way. Here are some examples:

> I name this ship *Liberté*.
>
> I apologize.
>
> I welcome you.
>
> I advise you to do it.

From *Philosophy and Ordinary Language,* edited by Charles E. Caton (University of Illinois Press, Urbana, 1963), pp. 22–23. Reprinted by permission of Mrs. J. Austin, G. J. Warnock and the University of Illinois Press.

[1] [Not here reprinted. Ed.]

[2] [The French term is '*assertion*'. I am sure that 'statement' is the English term Austin would have used here, and I have so translated '*assertion*' throughout. Trans.]

[3] ['*Formuler un tel énoncé*'. The translation is supplied in a footnote by Austin himself. Trans.]

Utterances of this kind are common enough: we find them, for instance, every-where in what are called in English the 'operative' clauses of a legal instrument.[4] Plainly, many of them are not without interest for philosophers: to say 'I promise to . . .'—to issue, as we say, this performative utterance—just *is* the act of making a promise; not, as we see, at all a mysterious act. And it may seem at once quite obvious that an utterance of this kind can't be true or false—notice that I say it can't *be* true or false, because it may very well *imply* that some *other* propositions are true or are false, but that, if I'm not mistaken, is a quite different matter.

However, the performative utterance is not exempt from all criticism: it may very well be criticized, but in a quite different dimension from that of truth and falsity. The performative must be issued in a situation appropriate in all respects for the act in question: if the speaker is not in the conditions required for its performance (and there are many such conditions), then his utterance will be, as we call it in general, 'unhappy'.[5]

First, our performative, like any other ritual or ceremony, may be, as the lawyers say, 'null and void'. If, for example, the speaker is not in a position to perform an act of that kind, or if the object with respect to which he purports to perform it is not suitable for the purpose, then he doesn't manage, simply by issuing his utterance, to carry out the purported act. Thus a bigamist doesn't get married a second time, he only 'goes through the form' of a second marriage; I can't name the ship if I am not the person properly authorized to name it; and I can't quite bring off the baptism of penguins, those creatures being scarcely susceptible of that exploit.

Second, a performative utterance may be, though not void, 'unhappy' in a different way—if, that is, it is issued *insincerely*. If I say 'I promise to . . .' without in the least intending to carry out the promised action, perhaps even not believing that it is in my power to carry it out, the promise is hollow. It is made, certainly; but still, there is an 'unhappiness': I have *abused* the formula.

Let us now suppose that our act has been performed: everything has gone off quite normally, and also, if you like, sincerely. In that case, the performative utterance will characteristically 'take effect'. We do not mean by that that such-and-such a future event is or will be brought about as an effect of this action functioning as a cause. We mean rather that, in consequence of the performance of this act, such-and-such a future event, *if* it happens, will be *in order*, and such-and-such other events, *if* they happen, will not be in order. If I have said 'I promise', I shall not be in order if I break my word; if I have said 'I welcome you', I shall not be in order if I proceed to treat you as an enemy or an intruder. Thus we say that, even when the performa-tive has taken effect, there may always crop up a third kind of unhappiness, which we

[4] The clauses, that is to say, in which the legal act is actually performed, as opposed to those—the 'preamble'—which set out the circumstances of the transaction.

[5] ['Unhappy' is a term Austin regularly used in this connection, and he supplies it himself in brackets after the French '*malheureux*'. Trans.]

call 'breach of commitment'.[6] We may note also that commitments can be more or less vague, and can bind us in very different degrees.

There we have, then, three kinds of unhappiness associated with the performative utterance. It is possible to make a complete classification of these unhappinesses; but it must be admitted that, as practically goes without saying, the different kinds may not always be sharply distinguishable and may even coincide.[7] Then we must add that our performative is both an *action* and an *utterance*: so that, poor thing, it can't help being liable to be substandard in all the ways in which actions in general can be, as well as those in which utterances in general can be. For example, the performative may be issued under duress, or by accident; it may suffer from defective grammar, or from misunderstanding; it may figure in a context not wholly 'serious', in a play, perhaps, or in a poem. We leave all that on one side—let us simply bear in mind the more specific unhappiness of the performative, that is, nullity, abuse (insincerity), and breach of commitment.

Well, now that we have before us this idea of the performative, it is very natural to hope that we could proceed to find some criterion, whether of grammar or of vocabulary, which would make it possible for us to answer in every case the question whether a particular utterance is performative or not. But this hope is, alas, exaggerated and, in large measure, vain.

It is true that there exist two 'normal forms', so to speak, in which the performative finds expression. At first sight both of them, curiously enough, have a thoroughly constative look. One of these normal forms is that which I have already made use of in producing my examples: the utterance leads off with a verb in the first person singular of the present indicative active, as in 'I promise you that . . .'. The other form, which comes to exactly the same but is more common in utterances issued in writing, employs by contrast a verb in the *passive* voice and in the *second* or *third* person of the present indicative, as in 'Passengers are requested to cross the line by the footbridge only'. If we ask ourselves, as sometimes we may, whether a given utterance of this form is performative or constative, we may settle the question by asking whether it would be possible to insert in it the word 'hereby' or some equivalent—as, in French, the phrase '*par ces mots-ci*'.

By way of putting to the test utterances which one might take to be performative, we make use of a well-known asymmetry, in the case of what we call an 'explicit performative' verb, between the first person singular of the present indicative, and other persons and tenses of the same verb. Thus, 'I promise' is a formula which is used to perform the act of promising; 'I promised', on the other hand, or 'he promises', are expressions which serve simply to describe or report an act of promising, not to perform one.

---

[6] ['*Rupture d'engagement*'. Austin himself supplies the translation. Trans.]

[7] ['That is to say, a particular case of unhappiness might arguably, or even quite properly, be classifiable under more than one heading. Trans.]

However, it is not in the least necessary that an utterance, if it is to be performative, should be expressed in one of these so-called normal forms. To say 'Shut the door', plainly enough, is every bit as performative, every bit as much the performance of an act, as to say 'I order you to shut the door'. Even the word 'Dog' by itself can sometimes (at any rate in England, a country more practical than ceremonious) stand in place of an explicit and formal performative; one performs, by this little word, the very same act as by the utterance 'I warn you that the dog is about to attack us', or by 'Strangers are warned that here there is a vicious dog'. To make our utterance performative, and quite unambiguously so, we can make use, in place of the explicit formula, of a whole lot of more primitive devices such as intonation, for instance, or gesture; further, and above all, the very context in which the words are uttered can make it entirely certain how they are to be taken—as a description, for example, or again as a warning. Does this word 'Dog' just give us a bit of detail about the local fauna? In the context—when confronted, that is, with the notice on the gate— we just don't need to ask ourselves that question at all.

All we can really say is that our explicit performative formula ('I promise . . .', 'I order you . . .', etc.) serves to make explicit, and at the same time more precise, what act it is that the speaker purports to perform in issuing his utterance. I say 'to make explicit', and that is not at all the same thing as to *state*.[8] Bending low before you, I remove my hat, or perhaps I say 'Salaam'; then, certainly, I am doing obeisance to you, not just engaging in gymnastics; but the word 'Salaam' does not, any more than does the act of removing my hat, in any way *state* that I am doing obeisance to you. It is in this way that our formula *makes* the issuing of the utterance that action which it is, but does not *state* that it is that action.

The other forms of expression, those that have no explicit performative formula, will be more primitive and less precise, one might almost say more vague. If I say simply 'I will be there', there will be no telling, just by considering the words, whether I am taking on a commitment, or declaring an intention, or making perhaps a fatalistic prediction. One may think of the precise formulae as a relatively recent phenomenon in the evolution of language, and as going together with the evolution of more complex forms of society and science.

We can't, then, expect any purely verbal criterion of the performative. We may hope, all the same, that any utterance which is in fact performative will be reducible (in some sense of that word) to an utterance in one or the other of our normal forms. Then, going on from there, we should be able, with the help of a dictionary, to make a list of all the verbs which can figure in one of our explicit formulae. Thus we will achieve a useful classification of all the varieties of acts that we perform in saying something (in one sense, at least, of that ambiguous phrase).

We have now brought in, then, the ideas of the performative utterance, of its unhappinesses, and of its explicit formulae. But we have been talking all along as if

[8] ['*Affirmer*'. I have translated this verb by 'state' throughout. Trans.]

every utterance had to be *either* constative *or* performative, and as if the idea of the constative at any rate was as clear as it is familiar. But it is not.

Let us note in the first place that an utterance which is undoubtedly a statement of fact, therefore constative, can fail to get by[9] in more than one way. It can be untrue, to be sure; but it can also be absurd, and that not necessarily in some gross fashion (by being, for instance, ungrammatical). I would like to take a closer look at three rather more subtle ways of being absurd, two of which have only recently come to light.

(1) Someone says 'All John's children are bald, but [or 'and'] John has no children'; or perhaps he says 'All John's children are bald', when, as a matter of fact, John has no children.

(2) Someone says 'The cat is on the mat, but [or 'and'] I don't believe it is'; or perhaps he says 'The cat is on the mat', when, as a matter of fact, he does not believe it is.

(3) Someone says 'All the guests are French, and some of them aren't': or perhaps he says 'All the guests are French', and then afterwards says 'Some of the guests are not French'.

In each of these cases one experiences a feeling of outrage, and it's possible each time for us to try to express it in terms of the same word—'implication', or perhaps that word that we always find so handy, 'contradiction'. But there are more ways of killing the cat than drowning it in butter,[10] and equally, to do violence to language one does not always need a contradiction.

Let us use the three terms 'presuppose', 'imply', and 'entail'[11] for our three cases respectively. Then:

1. Not only 'John's children are bald', but equally 'John's children are not bald', presupposes that John has children. To talk about those children, or to refer to them, presupposes that they exist. By contrast, 'The cat is not on the mat' does *not*, equally with 'The cat is on the mat', imply that I believe it is; and similarly, 'None of the guests is French' does *not*, equally with 'All the guests are French', entail that it is false that some of the guests are not French.

2. We can quite well say 'It could be the case both that the cat is on the mat and that I do not believe it is'. That is to say, those two propositions are not in the least incompatible: both can be true together. What is impossible is to state both at the same time: his *stating* that the cat is on the mat is what implies that the speaker believes it is. By contrast, we couldn't say 'It could be the case both that John has no

---

[9] [The French phrase is 'peut ne pas jouer'. Austin himself sometimes used in English the coined term 'non-play' (see, e.g., *How To Do Things with Words*, pp. 18n. and 31), but in a more restricted sense than would be appropriate here. Trans.]

[10] English proverb. I am told that this rather refined way of disposing of cats is not found in France.

[11] [These three English terms are supplied in a footnote by Austin himself. Trans.]

children and that his children are bald'; just as we couldn't say 'It could be the case both that all the guests are French and that some of them are not French'.

3. If 'All the guests are French' entails 'It is not the case that some of the guests are not French', then 'Some of the guests are not French' entails 'It is not the case that all the guests are French'. It's a question here of the compatibility and incompatibility of propositions. By contrast, it isn't like this with presupposition: if 'John's children are bald' presupposes that John has children, it isn't true at all that 'John has no children' presupposes that John's children are not bald. Similarly, if 'The cat is on the mat' implies that I believe it is, it isn't true at all that to say 'I don't believe that the cat is on the mat' implies that the cat is not on the mat (not, at any rate, in the same sense of 'implies'; besides, we have already seen that 'implication', for us, is not a matter of the incompatibility of propositions).

Here then are three ways in which a statement can fail to get by without being untrue, and without being a sheer rigmarole either. I would like to call attention to the fact that these three ways of failing to get by correspond to three of the ways in which a performative utterance may be unhappy. To bring out the comparison, let's first take two performative utterances:

4. 'I bequeath my watch to you, but [or 'and'] I haven't got a watch'; or perhaps someone says 'I bequeath my watch to you' when he hasn't got a watch.

5. 'I promise to be there, but [or 'and'] I have no intention of being there'; or perhaps someone says 'I promise to be there' when he doesn't intend to be there.

We compare case 4 with case 1, the case, that is, of presupposition. For to say either 'I bequeath my watch to you' or 'I don't bequeath my watch to you' presupposes equally that I have a watch; that the watch exists is presupposed by the fact that it is spoken of or referred to, in the performative utterance just as much as in the constative utterance. And just as we can make use here of the term 'presupposition' as employed in the doctrine of the constative, equally we can take over for that doctrine the term 'void' as employed in the doctrine of the unhappinesses of the performative. The statement on the subject of John's children is, we may say, 'void for lack of reference', which is exactly what lawyers would say about the purported bequest of the watch. So here is a first instance in which a trouble that afflicts statements turns out to be identical with one of the unhappinesses typical of the performative utterance.

We compare case 5 with case 2, that is, the case where something is 'implied'. Just as my saying that the cat is on the mat implies that I believe it is, so my saying I promise to be there implies that I intend to be there. The procedure of stating is designed for those who honestly believe what they say, exactly as the procedure of promising is designed for those who have a certain intention, namely, the intention to do whatever it may be that they promise. If we don't hold the belief, or again don't have the intention, appropriate to the content of our utterance, then in each case there is lack of sincerity and abuse of the procedure. If, at the same time as we make the statement or the promise, we announce in the same breath that we don't believe it or we don't intend to, then the utterance is 'self-voiding', as we might call it; and hence our feeling of outrage on hearing it. Another instance, then, where a trouble which afflicts statements is identical with one of the unhappinesses which afflict performative utterances.

Let us look back, next, to case 3, the case of entailment among statements. Can we find, in the case of performatives, some analogue for this as well? When I make the statement, for instance, 'All the guests are French', do I not commit myself in a more or less rigorous fashion to behaving in future in such-and-such a way, in particular with respect to the statements I will make? If, in the sequel, I state things incompatible with my utterance (namely, that all the guests are French), there will be a breach of commitment that one might well compare with that of the case in which I say 'I welcome you', and then proceed to treat you as an enemy or an intruder—and perhaps even better, with that of which one is guilty when one says 'I define the word thus' (a performative utterance) and then proceeds to use the word with a different meaning.

So then, it seems to me that the constative utterance is every bit as liable to unhappinesses as the performative utterance, and indeed to pretty much the same unhappinesses. Furthermore, making use of the key provided by our list of un- happinesses noted for the case of performatives, we can ask ourselves whether there are not still more unhappinesses in the case of statements, besides the three we have just mentioned. For example, it often happens that a performative is void because the utterer is not in a state, or not in a position, to perform the act which he purports to perform; thus, it's no good my saying 'I order you' if I have no authority over you: I can't order you, my utterance is void, my act is only purported. Now people have, I know, the impression that where a statement, a constative utterance, is in question, the case is quite different: anybody at all can state anything at all. What if he's ill-informed? Well then, one can be mistaken, that's all. It's a free country, isn't it? To state what isn't true is one of the Rights of Man. However, this impression can lead us into error. In reality nothing is more common than to find that one can state absolutely nothing on some subject, because one is simply not in a position to state whatever it may be—and this may come about, too, for more than one reason. I *cannot* state at this moment how many people there are in the next room: I haven't been to see, I haven't found out the facts. What if I say, nevertheless, 'At this moment there are fifty people in the next room'? You will allow, perhaps, that in saying that I have made a guess,[12] but you will not allow that I have made a statement, not at any rate without adding 'but he had no right whatever to do so'; and in this case my 'I

---

[12] [The French text has '*conjoncture*' here, but this must surely be a misprint for '*conjecture*'. Trans.]

state . . .' is exactly on a par with our 'I order . . .', said, we remember, without any right to give an order. Here's another example. You confide to me 'I'm bored', and I quite coolly reply 'You're not'. You say 'What do you mean, I'm not? What right have you to say how I feel?' I say 'But what do *you* mean, what right have I? I'm just stating what your feelings are, that's all. I may be mistaken, certainly, but what of that? I suppose one can always make a simple statement, can't one?' But no, one can't always: usually, I can't state what your feelings are, unless you have disclosed them to me.

So far I have called attention to two things: that there is no purely verbal criterion by which to distinguish the performative from the constative utterance, and that the constative is liable to the same unhappinesses as the performative. Now we must ask ourselves whether issuing a constative utterance is not, after all, the performance of an act, the act, namely, of stating. Is stating an act in the same sense as marrying, apologizing, betting, etc.? I can't plumb this mystery any further at present. But it is already pretty evident that the formula 'I state that . . .' is closely similar to the formula 'I warn you that . . .'—a formula which, as we put it, serves to make explicit what speech-act[13] it is that we are performing; and also, that one can't issue any utterance whatever without performing some speech-act of this kind.

What we need, perhaps, is a more general theory of these speech-acts, and in this theory our Constative-Performative antithesis will scarcely survive.

Here and now it remains for us to examine, quite briefly, this craze for being either true or false, something which people think is peculiar to statements alone and ought to be set up on a pedestal of its own, above the battle. And this time let's begin with the performative utterance: is it the case that there is nothing here in the least analogous with truth?

To begin with, it is clear that if we establish that a performative utterance is not unhappy, that is, that its author has performed his act happily and in all sincerity, that still does not suffice to set it beyond the reach of all criticism. It may always be criticized in a different dimension.

Let us suppose that I say to you 'I advise you to do it'; and let us allow that all the circumstances are appropriate, the conditions for success are fulfilled. In saying that, I actually do advise you to do it—it is not that I *state*, truely or falsely, *that* I advise you. It is, then, a performative utterance. There does still arise, all the same, a little question: was the advice good or bad? Agreed, I spoke in all sincerity, I believed that to do it would be in your interest; but was I right? Was my belief, in these circumstances, justified? Or again—though perhaps this matters less—was it in fact, or as things turned out, in your interest? There is confrontation of my utterance with the situation in, and the situation with respect to which, it was issued. I was fully justified perhaps, but was I right?

Many other utterances which have an incontestably performative flavour are

---

[13] [Austin supplies this English term himself. It is in any case the term he regularly used. Trans.]

exposed to this second kind of criticism. Allowing that, in declaring the accused guilty, you have reached your verdict properly and in good faith, it still remains to ask whether the verdict was just, or fair. Allowing that you had the right to reprimand him as you did, and that you have acted without malice, one can still ask whether your reprimand was deserved. Here again we have confrontation with the facts, including the circumstances of the occasion of utterance.

That not all performative utterances without exception are liable to this quasi-objective evaluation—which for that matter must here be left pretty vague and multifarious—may very well be true.

There is one thing that people will be particularly tempted to bring up as an objection against any comparison between this second kind of criticism and the kind appropriate to statements, and that is this: aren't these questions about something's being good, or just, or fair, or deserved entirely distinct from questions of truth and falsehood? That, surely, is a very simple black-and-white business: either the utterance corresponds to the facts or it doesn't, and that's that.

Well, I for my part don't think it is. Even if there exists a well-defined class of statements and we can restrict ourselves to that, this class will always be pretty wide. In this class we shall have the following statements:

> France is hexagonal.
> Lord Raglan won the battle of Alma.
> Oxford is 60 miles from London.

It's quite true that for each of these statements we can raise the question 'true or false'. But it is only in quite favourable cases that we ought to expect an answer yes or no, once and for all. When the question is raised one understands that the utterance is to be confronted in one way or another with the facts. Very well. So let's confront 'France is hexagonal' with France. What are we to say, is it true or not? The question, plainly, oversimplifies things. Oh well, up to a point if you like, I see what you mean, true perhaps for some purposes or in some contexts, that would do for the the man in the street but not for geographers. And so on. It's a rough statement, no denying that, but one can't just say straight out that it's false. Then Alma, a soldier's battle if ever there was one; it's true that Lord Raglan was in command of the allied army, and that this army to some extent won a confused sort of victory; yes, that would be a fair judgement, even well deserved, for schoolchildren anyway, though really it's a bit of an exaggeration. And Oxford, well yes, it's true that that city is 60 miles from London, so long as you want only a certain degree of precision.

Under the heading 'truth' what we in fact have is, not a simple quality nor a relation, not indeed *one* anything, but rather a whole dimension of criticism. We can get some idea, perhaps not a very clear one, of this criticism; what *is* clear is that there is a whole lot of things to be considered and weighed up in this dimension alone—the facts, yes, but also the situation of the speaker, his purpose in speaking, his hearer, questions of precision, etc. If we are content to restrict ourselves to statements of an idiotic or ideal simplicity, we shall never succeed in disentangling the true from the just, fair, deserved, precise, exaggerated, etc., the summary and the detail, the full and the concise, and so on.

From this side also, then, from the side of truth and falsehood, we feel ourselves driven to think again about the Performative-Constative antithesis. What we need, it seems to me, is a new doctrine, both complete and general, of *what one is doing in saying something*, in all the senses of that ambiguous phrase, and of what I call the speech-act, not just in this or that aspect abstracting from all the rest, but taken in its totality.

INTENTION AND CONVENTION IN SPEECH ACTS

P. F. STRAWSON

I

IN this paper I want to discuss some questions regarding J. L. Austin's notions of the illocutionary force of an utterance and of the illocutionary act which a speaker performs in making an utterance.[1]

There are two preliminary matters I must mention, if only to get them out of the way. Austin contrasts what he calls the 'normal' or 'serious' use of speech with what he calls 'etiolated' or 'parasitical' uses. His doctrine of illocutionary force relates essentially to the normal or serious use of speech and not, or not directly, to etiolated or parasitical uses; and so it will be with my comments on his doctrine. I am not suggesting that the distinction between the normal or serious use of speech and the secondary uses which he calls etiolated or parasitical is so clear as to call for no further examination; but I shall take it that there is such a distinction to be drawn and I shall not here further examine it.

My second preliminary remark concerns another distinction, or pair of distinctions, which Austin draws. Austin distinguishes the illocutionary force of an utterance from what he calls its 'meaning' and distinguishes between the illocutionary and the locutionary acts performed in issuing the utterance. Doubts may be felt about the second term of each of these distinctions. It may be felt that Austin has not made clear just what abstractions from the total speech act he intends to make by means of his notions of meaning and of locutionary act. Although this is a question on which I have views, it is not what the present paper is about. Whatever doubts may be entertained about Austin's notions of meaning and of locutionary act, it is enough for present purposes to be able to say, as I think we clearly can, the following about their relation to the notion of illocutionary force. The meaning of a (serious) utterance, as conceived by Austin, always embodies some limitation on its possible force, and sometimes—as, for example, in some cases where an explicit performative formula, like 'I apologize', is used—the meaning of an utterance may exhaust its

From *The Philosophical Review*, vol. LXXIII, no. 4, October 1964, pp. 439–60. Reprinted by permission of the author and the editor of *Philosophical Review*.

[1] All references, unless otherwise indicated, are to *How To Do Things with Words* (Oxford, 1962).

force; that is, there may be no more to the force than there is to the meaning; but very often the meaning, though it limits, does not exhaust, the force. Similarly, there may sometimes be no more to say about the illocutionary force of an utterance than we already know if we know what locutionary act has been performed; but very often there is more to know about the illocutionary force of an utterance than we know in knowing what locutionary act has been performed.

So much for these two preliminaries. Now I shall proceed to assemble from the text some indications as to what Austin means by the force of an utterance and as to what he means by an illocutionary act. These two notions are not so closely related that to know the force of an utterance is the same thing as to know what illocutionary act was actually performed in issuing it. For if an utterance with the illocutionary force of, say, a warning is not understood in this way (that is, as a warning) by the audience to which it is addressed, then (it is held) the illocutionary act of warning cannot be said to have been actually performed. 'The performance of an illocutionary act involves the securing of uptake'; that is, it involves 'bringing about the understanding of the meaning and of the force of the locution' (pp. 115–16).[2] Perhaps we may express the relation by saying that to know the force of an utterance is the same thing as to know what illocutionary act, *if any*, was actually performed in issuing it. Austin gives many examples and lists of words which help us to form at least a fair intuitive notion of what is meant by 'illocutionary force' and 'illocutionary act'. Besides these, he gives us certain general clues to these ideas, which may be grouped, as follows, under four heads:

1. Given that we know (in Austin's sense) the meaning of an utterance, there may still be a further question as to *how what was said was meant* by the speaker, or as to *how the words spoken were used,* or as to *how the utterance was to be taken* or *ought to have been taken* (pp. 98–9). In order to know the illocutionary force of the utterance, we must know the answer to this further question.

2. A locutionary act is an act *of* saying something; an illocutionary act is an act we perform *in* saying something. It is what we *do, in* saying what we *say.* Austin does not regard this characterization as by any means a satisfactory test for identifying kinds of illocutionary acts since, so regarded, it would admit many kinds of acts which he wishes to exclude from the class (p. 99 and Lecture X).

3. It is a sufficient, thought not, I think, a necessary, condition of a verb's being the name of a *kind* of illocutionary act that it can figure, in the first person present indicative, as what Austin calls an explicit performative. (This latter notion I shall assume to be familiar and perspicuous.)

4. The illocutionary act is 'a conventional act; an act done as conforming to a convention' (p. 105). As such, it is to be sharply contrasted with the producing of certain effects, intended or otherwise, by means of an utterance. This producing of

---

[2] I refer later to the need for qualification of this doctrine.

effects, though it too can often be ascribed *as an act* to the speaker (his *perlocutionary* act), is in no way a conventional act (pp. 120–1). Austin reverts many times to the 'conventional' nature of the illocutionary act (pp. 103, 105, 108, 115, 120, 121, 127) and speaks also of 'conventions of illocutionary force' (p. 114). Indeed, he remarks (pp. 120–1) that though acts which can properly be called by the same names as illocutionary acts—for example, acts of warning—can be brought off nonverbally, without the use of words, yet, in order to be properly called by these names, such acts must be *conventional* nonverbal acts.

II

I shall assume that we are clear enough about the intended application of Austin's notions of illocutionary force and illocutionary act to be able to criticize, by reference to cases, his general doctrines regarding those notions. It is the general doctrine I listed last above—the doctrine that an utterance's having such and such a force is a matter of convention—that I shall take as the starting point of inquiry. Usually this doctrine is affirmed in a quite unqualified way. But just once there occurs an interestingly qualified statement of it. Austin says, of the use of language with a certain illocutionary force, that 'it may . . . be said to be *conventional* in the sense that at least it could be made explicit by the performative formula' (p. 103). The remark has a certain authority in that it is the first explicit statement of the conventional nature of the illocutionary act. I shall refer to it later.

Meanwhile let us consider the doctrine in its unqualified form. Why does Austin say that the illocutionary act is a conventional act, an act done as conforming to a convention? I must first mention, and neutralize, two possible sources of confusion. (It may seem an excess of precaution to do so. I apologize to those who find it so.) First, we may agree (or not dispute) that any speech act is, as such, at least in part a conventional act. The performance of any *speech* act involves at least the observance or exploitation of some *linguistic* conventions, and every illocutionary act is a speech act. But it is absolutely clear that this is not the point that Austin is making in declaring the illocutionary act to be a conventional act. We must refer, Austin would say, to linguistic conventions to determine what *locutionary* act has been performed in the making of an utterance, to determine what the *meaning* of the utterance is. The doctrine now before us is the further doctrine that where force is *not* exhausted by meaning, the fact that an utterance has the further unexhausted force it has is also a matter of convention; or, where it is exhausted by meaning, the fact *that* it is, is a matter of convention. It is not just as being a speech act that an illocutionary act— for example, of warning—is conventional. A nonverbal act of warning is, Austin maintains, conventionally such in just the same way as an illocutionary—that is, verbal—act of warning is conventionally such.

Second, we must dismiss as irrelevant the fact that it can properly be said to be a matter of convention that an act of, for example, warning is correctly called by this name. For if this were held to be a ground for saying that illocutionary acts were conventional acts, then any describable act whatever would, as correctly described, be a conventional act.

The contention that illocutionary force is a matter of convention is easily seen to be correct in a great number of cases. For very many kinds of human transaction involving speech are governed and in part constituted by what we easily recognize as established conventions of procedure additional to the conventions governing the *meanings* of our utterances. Thus the fact that the word 'guilty' is pronounced by the foreman of the jury in court at the proper moment constitutes his utterance as the act of bringing in a verdict; and that this is so is certainly a matter of the conventional procedures of the law. Similarly, it is a matter of convention that if the appropriate umpire pronounces a batsman 'out', he thereby performs the act of *giving the man out*, which no player or spectator shouting 'Out!' can do. Austin gives other examples, and there are doubtless many more which could be given, where there clearly exist statable conventions, relating to the circumstances of utterance, such that an utterance with a certain meaning, pronounced by the appropriate person in the appropriate circumstances, has the force it has *as* conforming to those conventions. Examples of illocutionary acts of which this is true can be found not only in the sphere of social institutions which have a legal point (like the marriage ceremony and the law courts themselves) or of activities governed by a definite set of rules (like cricket and games generally) but in many other relations of human life. The act of *introducing*, performed by uttering the words 'This is Mr. Smith', may be said to be an act performed as conforming to a convention. The act of surrendering, performed by saying '*Kamerad!*' and throwing up your arms when confronted with a bayonet, may be said to be (to have become) an act performed as conforming to an accepted convention, a conventional act.

But it seems equally clear that, although the circumstances of utterance are always relevant to the determination of the illocutionary force of an utterance, there are many cases in which it is not as conforming to an accepted *convention* of any kind (other than those linguistic conventions which help to fix the meaning of the utterance) that an illocutionary act is performed. It seems clear, that is, that there are many cases in which the illocutionary force of an utterance, though not exhausted by its meaning, is not owed to any *conventions* other than those which help to give it its meaning. Surely there may be cases in which to utter the words 'The ice over there is very thin' to a skater is to issue a warning (is to say something with the *force* of a warning) without its being the case that there is any statable convention at all (other than those which bear on the nature of the *locutionary* act) such that the speaker's act can be said to be an act done as conforming to that convention.

Here is another example. We can readily imagine circumstances in which an utterance of the words 'Don't go' would be correctly described not as a request or an order, but as an entreaty. I do not want to deny that there may be conventional postures or procedures for entreating: one can, for example, kneel down, raise one's arms and *say*, 'I entreat you.' But I do want to deny that an act of entreaty can be performed only as conforming to some such conventions. What makes *X*'s words to *Y* an *entreaty* not to go is something—complex enough, no doubt—relating to *X*'s situation, attitude to *Y*, manner, and current intention. There are questions here which we must discuss later. But to suppose that there is always and necessarily a convention conformed to would be like supposing that there could be no love affairs which did not proceed on lines laid down in the *Roman de la Rose* or that every dispute between men must follow the pattern specified in Touchstone's speech about the countercheck quarrelsome and the lie direct.

Another example. In the course of a philosophical discussion (or, for that matter, a debate on policy) one speaker *raises an objection* to what the previous speaker has just said. *X* says (or proposes) that *p* and *Y objects* that *q*. *Y*'s utterance has the force of an objection to *X*'s assertion (or proposal) that *p*. But where is the *convention* that constitutes it an objection? That *Y*'s utterance has the force of an objection may lie partly in the character of the dispute and of *X*'s contention (or proposal) and it certainly lies partly, in *Y*'s *view* of these things, in the bearing which he takes the proposition that *q* to have on the doctrine (or proposal) that *p*. But although there may be, there does not have to be, any convention involved other than those linguistic conventions which help to fix the meanings of the utterances.

I do not think it necessary to give further examples. It seems perfectly clear that, if at least we take the expressions 'convention' and 'conventional' in the most natural way, the doctrine of the conventional nature of the illocutionary act does not hold generally. Some illocutionary acts are conventional; others are not (except in so far as they are locutionary acts). Why then does Austin repeatedly affirm the contrary? It is unlikely that he has made the simple mistake of generalizing from some cases to all. It is much more likely that he is moved by some further, and fundamental, feature of illocutionary acts, which it must be our business to discover. Even though we may decide that the description 'conventional' is not appropriately used, we may presume it worth our while to look for the reason for using it. Here we may recall that oddly qualified remark that the performance of an illocutionary act, or the use of a sentence with a certain illocutionary force, 'may be said to be conventional in the sense that at least it *could* be made explicit by the performative formula' (p. 103). On this we may first, and with justice, be inclined to comment that there is no such *sense* of 'being conventional', that if this is a *sense* of anything to the purpose, it is a sense of 'being *capable* of being conventional'. But although this is a proper comment on the remark, we should not simply dismiss the remark with this comment. Whatever it is that leads Austin to call illocutionary acts in general 'conventional' must be closely connected with whatever it is about such acts as warning, entreating, apologizing, advising, that accounts for the fact that *they* at least *could* be made explicit by the use of the corresponding first-person performative form. So we must ask what it is about them that accounts for this fact. Obviously it will not do to answer simply that they are acts which can be performed by the use of words. So are many (perlocutionary) acts, like convincing, dissuading, alarming, and amusing, for which, as Austin points out, there is no corresponding first-person *performative* formula. So we need some further explanation.

III

I think a concept we may find helpful at this point is one introduced by H. P. Grice in his valuable article on *Meaning (Philosophical Review,* LXVII, 1957), namely, the concept of *someone's nonnaturally meaning something by an utterance.* The concept does not apply only to speech acts—that is, to cases where that by which someone nonnaturally means something is a *linguistic* utterance. It is of more general application. But it will be convenient to refer to that by which someone, S, nonnaturally means something as S's *utterance.* The explanation of the introduced concept is given in terms of the concept of intention. S nonnaturally means something by an utterance x if S intends (i_1) to produce by uttering x a certain response (r) in an audience A and intends (i_2) that A shall recognize S's intention (i_1) and intends (i_3) that this recognition on the part of A of S's intention (i_1) shall function as A's reason, or a part of his reason, for his response r. (The word 'response', though more convenient in some ways than Grice's 'effect', is not ideal. It is intended to cover cognitive and affective states or attitudes as well as actions.) It is, evidently, an important feature of this definition that the securing of the response r is intended to be mediated by the securing of another (and always cognitive) effect in A; namely, recognition of S's intention to secure response r.

Grice's analysis of his concept is fairly complex. But I think a little reflection shows that it is not quite complex enough for his purpose. Grice's analysis is undoubtedly offered as an analysis of a situation in which one person is trying, in a sense of the word 'communicate' fundamental to any theory of meaning, to communicate with another. But it is possible to imagine a situation in which Grice's three conditions would be satisfied by a person S and yet, in this important sense of 'communicate', it would not be the case that S could be said to be trying to communicate by means of his production of x with the person A in whom he was trying to produce the response r. I proceed to describe such a situation.

S intends by a certain action to induce in A the belief that p; so he satisfies condition (i_1). He arranges convincing-looking 'evidence' that p, in a place where A is bound to see it. He does this, knowing that A is watching him at work, but *knowing also that* A *does not know that* S *knows that* A *is watching him at work.* He realizes that A will not take the *arranged* 'evidence' as genuine or natural evidence that p, but realizes, and indeed intends, that A will take his arranging of it as grounds for thinking that he, S, intends to induce in A the belief that p. That is, he intends A to recognize his (i_1) intention. So S satisfies condition (i_2). He knows that A has general grounds for thinking that S would not wish to make him, A, think that p unless it were known to S to be the case that p; and hence that A's recognition of his (S's) intention to induce in A the belief that p will in fact seem to A a sufficient reason for believing that p. And he intends that A's recognition of his intention (i_1) should function in just this way. So he satisfies condition (i_3).

S, then, satisfies all Grice's conditions. But this is clearly not a case of attempted *communication* in the sense which (I think it is fair to assume) Grice is seeking to elucidate. A will indeed take S to be trying to bring it about that A is aware of some fact; but he will not take S as trying, in the colloquial sense, to 'let him know' something (or to 'tell' him something). But unless S at least brings it about that A takes him (S) to be trying to let him (A) know something, he has not succeeded in communicating with A; and if, as in our example, he has not even *tried* to bring this about, then he has not even *tried* to communicate with A. It seems a minimum further condition of his trying to do this that he should not only intend A to recognize his intention to get A to think that p, but that he should also *intend* A *to recognize his intention to get* A *to recognize his intention* to get A to think that p.

We might approximate more closely to the communication situation if we changed the example by supposing it not only clear to both A and S that A was watching S at work, but also clear to them both that it *was* clear to them both. I shall content myself, however, with drawing from the actually considered example the conclusion that we must add to Grice's conditions the further condition that S should have the further intention (i_4) that A should recognize his intention (i_2). It is possible that further argument could be produced to show that even adding this condition is not *sufficient* to constitute the case as one of attempted communication. But I shall rest content for the moment with the fact that this addition at least is necessary.

Now we might have expected in Grice's paper an account of what it is for A to *understand* something by an utterance x, an account complementary to the account of what it is for S to *mean* something by an utterance x. Grice in fact gives no such account, and I shall suggest a way of at least partially supplying this lack. I say 'at least partially' because the uncertainty as to the sufficiency of even the modified conditions for S's nonnaturally *meaning* something by an utterance x is reflected in a corresponding uncertainty in the sufficiency of conditions for A's understanding. But again we may be content for the moment with necessary conditions. I suggest, then, that for A (in the appropriate sense of 'understand') to understand *something* by utterance x, it is necessary (and perhaps sufficient) that there should be *some* complex intention of the (i_2) form, described above, which A takes S to have, and that for A to understand the utterance correctly, it is necessary that A should take S to have *the* complex intention of the (i_2) form which S does have. In other words, if A is to understand the utterance correctly, S's (i_4) intention and hence his (i_2) intention must be fulfilled. Of course it does not follow from the fulfilment of these intentions that his (i_1) intention is fulfilled; nor, consequently, that his (i_3) intention is fulfilled.

It is at this point, it seems, that we may hope to find a possible point of connection with Austin's terminology of 'securing uptake'. If we do find such a point of connection, we also find a possible starting point for an at least partial analysis of the notions of illocutionary force and of the illocutionary act. For to secure uptake is to secure understanding of (meaning and) illocutionary force; and securing understanding of illocutionary force is said by Austin to be an essential element in bringing off the illocutionary act. It is true that this doctrine of Austin's may be objected to.[3] For surely a man may, for example, actually have made such and such a bequest, or gift, even if no one ever reads his will or instrument of gift. We may be tempted to say instead that at least *the aim, if not the achievement*, of securing uptake is an essential element in the performance of the illocutionary act. To this, too, there is an objection. Might not a man really have made a gift, in due form, and take some satisfaction in the thought, even if he had no expectations of the fact ever being known? But this objection at most forces on us an amendment to which we are in any case obliged[4]: namely, that the aim, if not the achievement, of securing uptake is essentially *a standard, if not an invariable,* element in the performance of the illocutionary act. So the analysis of the aim of securing uptake remains an essential element in the analysis of the notion of the illocutionary act.

IV

Let us, then, make a tentative identification—to be subsequently qualified and revised —of Austin's notion of uptake with that at least partially analysed notion of understanding (on the part of an audience) which I introduced just now as complementary to Grice's concept of somebody nonnaturally meaning something by an utterance. Since the notion of audience understanding is introduced by way of a fuller (though partial) analysis than any which Austin gives of the notion of uptake, the identification is equivalent to a tentative (and partial) analysis of the notion of uptake and hence of the notions of illocutionary act and illocutionary force. If the identification were correct, then it would follow that to say something with a certain illocutionary force is at least (in the standard case) to have a certain complex intention of the (i_4) form described in setting out and modifying Grice's doctrine.

Next we test the adequacy and explanatory power of this partial analysis by seeing how far it helps to explain other features of Austin's doctrine regarding illocutionary acts. There are two points at which we shall apply this test. One is the point at which Austin maintains that the production of an utterance with a certain illocutionary

---

[3] I owe the objections which follow to Professor Hart.

[4] For an illocutionary act *may* be performed *altogether* unintentionally. See the example about redoubling at bridge, p. 36 below.

force is a conventional act in that unconventional sense of 'conventional' which he glosses in terms of general suitability for being made explicit with the help of an explicitly performative formula. The other is the point at which Austin considers the possibility of a general characterization of the illocutionary act as what we *do*, *in* saying what we say. He remarks on the unsatisfactoriness of this characterization in that it would admit as illocutionary acts what are not such; and we may see whether the suggested analysis helps to explain the exclusion from the class of illocutionary acts of those acts falling under this characterization which Austin wishes to exclude. These points are closely connected with each other.

First, then, we take the point about the general suitability of an illocutionary act for performance with the help of the explicitly performative formula for that act. The explanation of this feature of illocutionary acts has two phases; it consists of, first, a general, and then a special, point about intention. The first point may be roughly expressed by saying that in general a man can speak of his intention in performing an action with a kind of authority which he cannot command in predicting its outcome. What he intends in doing something is up to him in a way in which the results of his doing it are not, or not only, up to him. But we are concerned not with just any intention to produce any kind of effect by acting, but with a very special kind of case. We are concerned with the case in which there is not simply an intention to produce a certain response in an audience, but an intention to produce that response by means of recognition on the part of the audience of the intention to produce that response, this recognition to serve as part of the reason that the audience has for its response, and the intention that this recognition should occur being itself intended to be recognized. The speaker, then, not only has the general authority on the subject of his intention that any agent has; he also has a motive, inseparable from the nature of his act, for making that intention clear. For he will not have secured understanding of the illocutionary force of his utterance, he will not have performed the act of communication he sets out to perform, unless his complex intention is grasped. Now clearly, for the enterprise to be possible at all, there must exist, or he must find, means of making the intention clear. If there exists any conventional linguistic means of doing so, the speaker has both a right to use, and a motive for using, those means. One such means, available sometimes, which comes very close to the employment of the explicit performative form, would be to attach, or subjoin, to the substance of the message what looks like a force-elucidating *comment* on it, which may or may not have the form of a self-ascription. Thus we have phrases like 'This is only a suggestion' or 'I'm only making a suggestion'; or again 'That was a warning' or 'I'm warning you'. For using such phrases, I repeat, the speaker has the *authority* that anyone has to speak on the subject of his intentions and the *motive* that I have tried to show is inseparable from an act of communication.

From such phrases as these—which have, *in appearance*, the character of comments on utterances other than themselves—to the explicit performative formula the step is only a short one. My reason for *qualifying* the remark that such phrases have the character of comments on utterances other than themselves is this. We are considering the case in which the subjoined quasi-comment is addressed to the same audience as the utterance on which it is a quasi-comment. Since it is *part* of the speaker's audience-directed intention to make clear the character of his utterance as, for example, a warning, and since the subjoined quasi-comment directly subserves this intention, it is better to view the case, appearances notwithstanding, *not* as a case in which we have two utterances, one commenting on the other, but as a case of a single unitary speech act. Crudely, the addition of the quasi-comment 'That was a warning' is *part* of the total act of warning. The effect of the short step to the explicitly performative formula is simply to bring appearances into line with reality. When that short step is taken, we no longer have, even in appearance, two utterances, one a comment on the other, but a single utterance in which the first-person performative verb *manifestly* has that peculiar logical character of which Austin rightly made so much, and which we may express in the present context by saying that the verb serves not exactly to *ascribe* an intention to the speaker but rather, in Austin's phrase, to *make explicit* the type of communication intention with which the speaker speaks, the type of force which the utterance has.

The above might be said to be a deduction of the general possibility and utility of the explicitly performative formula for the cases of illocutionary acts not essentially conventional. It may be objected that the deduction fails to show that the intentions rendered explicit by the use of performative formulae *in general* must be of just the complex form described, and hence fails to justify the claim that just this kind of intention lies at the core of all illocutionary acts. And indeed we shall see that this claim would be mistaken. But before discussing why, we shall make a further application of the analysis at the second testing point I mentioned. That is, we shall see what power it has to explain why some of the things we may be *doing*, *in* saying what we say, are not illocutionary acts and could not be rendered explicit by the use of the performative formula.

Among the things mentioned by Austin which we might be doing in saying things, but which are not illocutionary acts, I shall consider the two examples of (1) showing off and (2) insinuating. Now when we show off, we are certainly trying to produce an effect on the audience: we talk, indeed, for effect; we try to impress, to evoke the response of admiration. But it is no part of the intention to secure the effect *by means of* the recognition of the intention to secure it. It is no part of our total intention to secure recognition of the intention to produce the effect at all. On the contrary: recognition of the intention might militate against securing the effect and promote an opposite effect, for example, disgust.

This leads on to a further general point not explicitly considered by Austin, but satisfactorily explained by the analysis under consideration. In saying to an audience what we do say, we very often intend not only to produce the primary response *r* by means of audience recognition of the intention to produce that response, but to produce further effects by means of the production of the primary response r. Thus my further purpose in informing you that p (that is, aiming to produce in you the primary cognitive response of knowledge or belief that p) may be to bring it about thereby that you adopt a certain line of conduct or a certain attitude. In saying what I say, then, part of what I am *doing* is trying to influence your attitudes or conduct in a certain way. Does this part of what I am doing in saying what I say contribute to determining the character of the illocutionary act I perform? And if not, why not? If we take the first question strictly as introduced and posed, the answer to it is 'No'. The reason for the answer follows from the analysis. We have no complex intention (i_4) that there should be recognition of an intention (i_2) that there should be recognition of an intention (i_1) that the further effect should be produced; for it is no part of our intention that the further effect should be produced by way of recognition of our intention that it should be; the production in the audience of belief that p is intended to be itself the means whereby his attitude or conduct is to be influenced. We secure uptake, perform the act of communication that we set out to perform, if the audience understands us as *informing* him that p. Although it is true that, in saying what we say, we are in fact *trying* to produce the further effect—this is part of what we are doing, whether we succeed in producing the effect or not—yet this does not enter into the characterization of the illocutionary act. With this case we have to contrast the case in which, instead of aiming at a primary response and a further effect, the latter to be secured through the former alone, we aim at a complex primary response. Thus in the case where I do not simply inform, but warn, you that p, among the intentions I intend you to recognize (and intend you to recognize as intended to be recognized), are not only the intention to secure your belief that p, but the intention to secure that you are on your guard against p-perils. The difference (one of the differences) between showing off and warning is that your recognition of my intention to put you on your guard may well contribute to putting you on your guard, whereas your recognition of my intention to impress you is not likely to contribute to my impressing you (or not in the way I intended).[5]

Insinuating fails, for a different reason, to be a type of illocutionary act. An essential feature of the intentions which make up the illocutionary complex is their overtness. They have, one might say, essential avowability. This is, in one respect, a logically embarrassing feature. We have noticed already how we had to meet the threat of a counterexample to Grice's analysis of the communicative act in terms of three types of intention—(i_1), (i_2), and (i_3)—by the addition of a further intention (i_4) that an intention (i_2) should be recognized. We have no proof, however, that the

---

[5] Perhaps trying to impress might sometimes have an illocutionary character. For I might try to impress you with my *effrontery*, intending you to recognize this intention and intending your recognition of it to function as part of your reason for being impressed, and so forth. But then I am not *merely* trying to impress you; I am *inviting* you to be impressed. I owe this point to Mr. B. F. McGuinness.

resulting enlarged set of conditions is a complete analysis. Ingenuity might show it was not; and the way seems open to a regressive series of intentions that intentions should be recognized. While I do not think there is anything necessarily objectionable in this, it does suggest that the complete and rounded-off set of conditions aimed at in a conventional analysis is not easily and certainly attainable in these terms. That is why I speak of the feature in question in these terms. That is why I speak of the feature in question as logically embarrassing. At the same time it enables us easily to dispose of insinuating as a candidate for the status of a type of illocutionary act. The whole point of insinuating is that the audience is to *suspect*, but not more than suspect, the intention, for example, to induce or disclose a certain belief. The intention one has in insinuating is essentially nonavowable.

Now let us take stock a little. We tentatively laid it down as a necessary condition of securing understanding of the illocutionary force of an utterance that the speaker should succeed in bringing it about that the audience took him, in issuing his utterance, to have a complex intention of a certain kind, namely the intention that the audience should recognize (and recognize as intended to be recognized) his intention to induce a certain response in the audience. The suggestion has, as we have just seen, certain explanatory merits. Nevertheless we cannot claim general application for it as even a partial analysis of the notions of illocutionary force and illocutionary act. Let us look at some reasons why not.

V

I remarked earlier that the words 'Don't go' may have the force, *inter alia*, either of a request or of an entreaty. In either case the primary intention of the utterance (if we presume the words to be uttered with the *sense* 'Don't go *away*') is that of inducing the person addressed to stay where he is. His staying where he is is the primary response aimed at. But the only other intentions mentioned in our scheme of partial analysis relate directly or indirectly to recognition of the primary intention. So how, in terms of that scheme, are we to account for the variation in illocutionary force between requests and entreaties?

This question does not appear to raise a major difficulty for the scheme. The scheme, it seems, merely requires supplementing and enriching. *Entreaty*, for example, is a matter of trying to secure the primary response not merely through audience recognition of the intention to secure it, but through audience recognition of a complex attitude of which this primary intention forms an integral part. A wish that someone should stay may be held in different ways: passionately or lightly, confidently or desperately; and it may, for different reasons, be part of a speaker's intention to secure recognition of *how* he holds it. The most obvious reason, in the case of entreaty, is the belief, or hope, that such a revelation is more likely to secure the fulfilment of the primary intention.

But one may not only request and entreat; one may *order* someone to stay where he is. The words 'Don't go' may have the illocutionary force of an order. Can we so simply accommodate in our scheme *this* variation in illocutionary force? Well, we can accommodate it; though not so simply. We can say that a man who issues an order typically intends his utterance to secure a certain response, that he intends this intention to be recognized, and its recognition to be a reason for the response, that he intends the utterance to be recognized as issued in a certain social context such that certain social rules or conventions apply to the issuing of utterances in this context and such that certain consequences may follow in the event of the primary response not being secured, that he intends *this* intention too to be recognized, and finally that he intends the recognition of these last features to function as an element in the reasons for the response on the part of the audience.

Evidently, in this case, unlike the case of entreaty, the scheme has to be extended to make room for explicit reference to social convention. It can, with some strain, be so extended. But as we move further into the region of institutionalized procedures, the strain becomes too much for the scheme to bear. On the one hand, one of its basic features—namely, the reference to an intention to secure a definite response in an audience (over and above the securing of uptake)—has to be dropped. On the other, the reference to social conventions of procedure assumes a very much greater importance. Consider an umpire giving a batsman out, a jury bringing in a verdict of guilty, a judge pronouncing sentence, a player redoubling at bridge, a priest or a civil officer pronouncing a couple man and wife. Can we say that the umpire's primary intention is to secure a certain response (say, retiring to the pavilion) from a certain audience (say, the batsman), the jurymen's to secure a certain response (say, the pronouncing of sentence) from a certain audience (say, the judge), and then build the rest of our account around this, as we did, with some strain, in the case of the order? Not with plausibility. It is not even possible, in other than a formal sense, to isolate, among all the participants in the procedure (trial, marriage, game) to which the utterance belongs, a particular audience to whom the utterance can be said to be addressed.

Does this mean that the approach I suggested to the elucidation of the notion of illocutionary force is entirely mistaken? I do not think so. Rather, we must distinguish types of case; and then see what, if anything, is common to the types we have distinguished. What we initially take from Grice—with modifications—is an at least partially analytical account of an act of communication, an act which might indeed be performed nonverbally and yet exhibit all the essential characteristics of a (nonverbal) equivalent of an illocutionary act. We gain more than this. For the account enables us to understand how such an act may be linguistically conventionalized right up to the point at which illocutionary force is exhausted by meaning (in Austin's sense); and in this understanding the notion of wholly overt or essentially avowable intention plays an essential part. Evidently, in these cases, the illocutionary act itself is not *essentially* a conventional act, an act done as conforming to a convention; it may be that the act is conventional, done as conforming to a convention, only in so far as *the means used to perform it* are conventional. To speak only of those conventional means which are also *linguistic* means, the extent to which the act is one done as conforming to conventions may depend solely on the extent to which conventional linguistic meaning exhausts illocutionary force.

At the other end of the scale—the end, we may say, from which Austin began—we have illocutionary acts which *are* essentially conventional. The examples I mentioned just now will serve—marrying, redoubling, giving out, pronouncing sentence, bringing in a verdict. Such acts could have no existence outside the rule- or convention-governed practices and procedures of which they essentially form parts. Let us take the standard case in which the participants in these procedures know the rules and their roles, and are trying to play the game and not wreck it. Then they are presented with occasions on which they have to, or may, perform an illocutionary act which forms part of, or furthers, the practice or procedure as a whole; and sometimes they have to make a decision within a restricted range of alternatives (for example, to pass or redouble, to pronounce sentence of imprisonment for some period not exceeding a certain limit). Between the case of such acts as these and the case of the illocutionary act not essentially conventional, there is an important likeness and an important difference. The likeness resides in the fact that, in the case of an utterance belonging to a convention-governed practice or procedure, the speaker's utterance is standardly *intended* to further, or affect the course of, the practice in question in some one of the alternative ways open, and intended to be recognized as so intended. I do not mean that such an act could *never* be performed *unintentionally*. A player might let slip the word 'redouble' without *meaning* to redouble; but if the circumstances are appropriate and the play strict, then he *has* redoubled (or he may be *held* to have redoubled). But a player who continually did this sort of thing would not be asked to play again, except by sharpers. Forms can take charge, in the absence of appropriate intention; but when they do, the case is *essentially* deviant or nonstandard. There is present in the standard case, that is to say, the same element of wholly overt and avowable intention as in the case of the act not essentially conventional.

The difference is a more complicated affair. We have, in these cases, an act which is conventional in two connected ways. First, if things go in accordance with the rules of the procedure in question, the act of furthering the practice in the way intended is an act required or permitted by those rules, an act done as falling under the rules. Second, the act is identified as the act it is just because it is performed by the utterance of a form of words conventional for the performance of that act. Hence the speaker's utterance is not only *intended* to further, or affect the course of, the practice in question in a certain conventional way; in the absence of any breach of the conventional conditions for furthering the procedure in this way, it cannot fail to do so.

And here we have the contrast between the two types of case. In the case of an illocutionary act of a kind not essentially conventional, the act of communication is performed if *uptake* is secured, if the utterance is taken to be issued with the complex overt intention with which it is issued. But even though the act of communication is performed, the wholly overt intention which lies at the core of the intention complex may, *without any breach of rules or conventions,* be frustrated. The audience response (belief, action, or attitude) may simply not be forthcoming. It is different with the utterance which forms part of a wholly convention-governed procedure. Granted that uptake is secured, then any frustration of the wholly overt intention of the utterance (the intention to further the procedure in a certain way) must be attributable to a breach of rule or convention. The speaker who abides by the conventions can avow-ably have the intention to further the procedure in the way to which his current linguistic act is conventionally appropriated *only* if he takes it that the conventional conditions for so furthering it are satisfied and hence takes it *that his utterance will not only reveal his intentions but give them effect.* There is nothing parallel to this in the case of the illocutionary act of a kind not essentially conventional. In both cases, we may say, speakers assume the responsibility for making their intentions overt. In one case (the case of the convention-constituted procedure) the speaker who uses the explicitly performative form also explicitly assumes the responsibility for making his overt intention effective. But in the other case the speaker cannot, in the speech act itself, explicitly assume any such responsibility. For there are no conditions which can conventionally guarantee the effectiveness of his overt intention. Whether it is effective or not is something that rests with his audience. In the one case, therefore, the explicitly performative form *may* be the name of the very act which is performed if and only if the speaker's overt intention is effective; but in the other case it cannot be the name of this act. But of course—and I shall recur to this thought—the sharp contrast I have here drawn between two extreme types of case must not blind us to the existence of intermediate types.

Acts belonging to convention-constituted procedures of the kind I have just re-ferred to form an important part of human communication. But they do not form the whole nor, we may think, the most fundamental part. It would be a mistake to take them as the model for understanding the notion of illocutionary force in general, as Austin perhaps shows some tendency to do when he both insists that the illocutionary act is essentially a conventional act and connects this claim with the possibility of making the act explicit by the use of the performative formula. It would equally be a mistake, as we have seen, to generalize the account of illocutionary force derived from Grice's analysis; for this would involve holding, falsely, that the complex overt intention manifested in any illocutionary act always includes the intention to secure a certain definite response or reaction in an audience over and above that which is necessarily secured if the illocutionary force of the utterance is understood. Never-theless, we can perhaps extract from our consideration of two contrasting types of case something which is common to them both and to all the other types which lie between them. For the illocutionary force of an utterance is essentially something that is intended to be understood. And the understanding of the force of an utterance in all cases involves recognizing what may be called broadly an audience-directed intention and recognizing it as wholly overt, as intended to be organized. It is perhaps this fact which lies at the base of the general possibility of the explicit performative formula; though, as we have seen, extra factors come importantly into play in the case of convention-constituted procedures.

Once this common element in all illocutionary acts is clear, we can readily acknowledge that the types of audience-directed intention involved may be very various and, also, that different types may be exemplified by one and the same utterance.

I have set in sharp contrast those cases in which the overt intention is simply to forward a definite and convention-governed practice (for example, a game) in a definite way provided for by the conventions or rules of the practice and those cases in which the overt intention includes that of securing a definite response (cognitive or practical) in an audience over and above that which is necessarily secured if uptake is secured. But there is something misleading about the sharpness of this contrast; and it would certainly be wrong to suppose that all cases fall clearly and neatly into one or another of these two classes. A speaker whose job it is to do so may offer information, instructions, or even advice, and yet be overtly indifferent as to whether or not his information is accepted as such, his instructions followed, or his advice taken. His wholly overt intention may amount to no more than that of making available—in a 'take it or leave it' spirit—to his audience the information or instructions or opinion in question; though again, in some cases, he may be seen as the mouthpiece, merely, of another agency to which may be attributed at least general intentions of the kind that can scarcely be attributed, in the particular case, to him. We should not find such complications discouraging; for we can scarcely expect a general account of linguistic communication to yield more than schematic outlines, which may almost be lost to view when every qualification is added which fidelity to the facts requires.

III

WHAT IS A SPEECH ACT?

J. R. SEARLE

I. INTRODUCTION

In a typical speech situation involving a speaker, a hearer, and an utterance by the speaker, there are many kinds of acts associated with the speaker's utterance. The speaker will characteristically have moved his jaw and tongue and made noises. In addition, he will characteristically have performed some acts within the class which includes informing or irritating or boring his hearers; he will further characteristically have performed some acts within the class which includes referring to Kennedy or Khruschchev or the North Pole; and he will also have performed acts within the class which includes making statements, asking questions, issuing commands, giving reports, greeting, and warning. The members of this last class are what Austin[1] called illocutionary acts and it is with this class that I shall be concerned in this paper, so the paper might have been called 'What is an Illocutionary Act?' I do not attempt to define the expression 'illocutionary act', although if my analysis of a particular illocutionary act succeeds it may provide the basis for a definition. Some of the English verbs and verb phrases associated with illocutionary acts are: state, assert, describe, warn, remark, comment, command, order, request, criticize, apologize, censure, approve, welcome, promise, express approval, and express regret. Austin claimed that there were over a thousand such expressions in English.

By way of introduction, perhaps I can say why I think it is of interest and importance in the philosophy of language to study speech acts, or, as they are sometimes called, language acts or linguistic acts. I think it is essential to any specimen of linguistic communication that it involve a linguistic act. It is not, as has generally been supposed, the symbol or word or sentence, or even the token of the symbol or word or sentence, which is the unit of linguistic communication, but rather it is the *production* of the token in the performance of the speech act that constitutes the basic unit of linguistic communication. To put this point more precisely, the production of the sentence token under certain conditions is the illocutionary act, and the illocutionary act is the minimal unit of linguistic communication.

From *Philosophy in America,* ed. Max Black (Allen & Unwin, 1965), pp. 221–39. Reprinted by permission of the author, Cornell University Press and George Allen & Unwin Ltd.

[1] J. L. Austin, *How To Do Things with Words* (Oxford, 1962).

I do not know how to *prove* that linguistic communication essentially involves acts but I can think of arguments with which one might attempt to convince someone who was sceptical. One argument would be to call the sceptic's attention to the fact that when he takes a noise or a mark on paper to be an instance of linguistic communication, as a message, one of the things that is involved in his so taking that noise or mark is that he should regard it as having been produced by a being with certain intentions. He cannot just regard it as a natural phenomenon, like a stone, a waterfall, or a tree. In order to regard it as an instance of linguistic communication one must suppose that its production is what I am calling a speech act. It is a logical presupposition, for example, of current attempts to decipher the Mayan hieroglyphs that we at least hypothesize that the marks we see on the stones were produced by beings more or less like ourselves and produced with certain kinds of intentions. If we were certain the marks were a consequence of, say, water erosion, then the question of deciphering them or even calling them hieroglyphs could not arise. To construe them under the category of linguistic communication necessarily involves construing their production as speech acts.

To perform illocutionary acts is to engage in a rule-governed form of behaviour. I shall argue that such things as asking questions or making statements are rule-governed in ways quite similar to those in which getting a base hit in baseball or moving a knight in chess are rule-governed forms of acts. I intend therefore to explicate the notion of an illocutionary act by stating a set of necessary and sufficient conditions for the performance of a particular kind of illocutionary act, and extracting from it a set of semantical rules for the use of the expression (or syntactic device) which marks the utterance as an illocutionary act of that kind. If I am successful in stating the conditions and the corresponding rules for even one kind of illocutionary act, that will provide us with a pattern for analysing other kinds of acts and consequently for explicating the notion in general. But in order to set the stage for actually stating conditions and extracting rules for performing an illocutionary act I have to discuss three other preliminary notions: *rules*, *propositions*, and *meaning*. I shall confine my discussion of these notions to those aspects which are essential to my main purposes in this paper, but, even so, what I wish to say concerning each of these notions, if it were to be at all complete, would require a paper for each; however, sometimes it may be worth sacrificing thoroughness for the sake of scope and I shall therefore be very brief.

II. RULES

In recent years there has been in the philosophy of language considerable discussion involving the notion of rules for the use of expressions. Some philosophers have even said that knowing the meaning of the word is simply a matter of knowing the rules for its use or employment. One disquieting feature of such discussions is that no philosopher, to my knowledge at least, has ever given anything like an adequate formulation of the rules for the use of even one expression. If meaning is a matter of rules of use, surely we ought to be able to state the rules for the use of expressions in a way which would explicate the meaning of those expressions. Certain other philosophers, dismayed perhaps by the failure of their colleagues to produce any rules, have denied the fashionable view that meaning is a matter of rules and have asserted that there are no semantical rules of the proposed kind at all. I am inclined to think that this scepticism is premature and stems from a failure to distinguish different sorts of rules, in a way which I shall now attempt to explain.

I distinguish between two sorts of rules: Some regulate antecedently existing forms of behaviour; for example, the rules of etiquette regulate interpersonal relationships, but these relationships exist independently of the rules of etiquette. Some rules on the other hand do not merely regulate but create or define new forms of behaviour. The rules of football, for example, do not merely regulate the game of football but as it were create the possibility of or define that activity. The activity of playing football is constituted by acting in accordance with these rules; football has no existence apart from these rules. I call the latter kind of rules constitutive rules and the former kind regulative rules. Regulative rules regulate a pre-existing activity, an activity whose existence is logically independent of the existence of the rules. Constitutive rules constitute (and also regulate) an activity the existence of which is logically dependent on the rules. [2]

Regulative rules characteristically take the form of or can be paraphrased as imperatives, e.g. 'When cutting food hold the knife in the right hand', or 'Officers are to wear ties at dinner'. Some constitutive rules take quite a different form, e.g. a checkmate is made if the king is attacked in such a way that no move will leave it unattacked; a touchdown is scored when a player crosses the opponents' goal line in possession of the ball while play is in progress. If our paradigms of rules are imperative regulative rules, such non-imperative constitutive rules are likely to strike us as extremely curious and hardly even as rules at all. Notice that they are almost tautological in character, for what the 'rule' seems to offer is a partial definition of 'checkmate' or 'touchdown'. But, of course, this quasi-tautological character is a necessary consequence of their being constitutive rules: the rules concerning touchdowns must define the notion of 'touchdown' in the same way that the rules concerning football define 'football'. That, for example, a touchdown can be scored in such and such ways and counts six points can appear sometimes as a rule, sometimes as an analytic truth; and that it can be construed as a tautology is a clue to the fact that the rule in question is a constitutive one. Regulative rules generally have the form 'Do X' or

[2] This distinction occurs in J. Rawls, 'Two Concepts of Rules', *Philosophical Review*, 1955, and J. R. Searle, 'How to Derive "Ought" from "Is"', *Philosophical Review*, 1964.

'If Y do X'. Some members of the set of constitutive rules have this form but some also have the form 'X counts as Y'.[3]

The failure to perceive this is of some importance in philosophy. Thus, e.g., some philosophers ask 'How can a promise create an obligation?' A similar question would be 'How can a touchdown create six points?' And as they stand both questions can only be answered by stating a rule of the form 'X counts as Y'.

I am inclined to think that both the failure of some philosophers to state rules for the use of expressions and the scepticism of other philosophers concerning the existence of any such rules stem at least in part from a failure to recognize the distinctions between constitutive and regulative rules. The model or paradigm of a rule which most philosophers have is that of a regulative rule, and if one looks in semantics for purely regulative rules one is not likely to find anything interesting from the point of view of logical analysis. There are no doubt social rules of the form 'One ought not to utter obscenities at formal gatherings', but that hardly seems a rule of the sort that is crucial in explicating the semantics of a language. The hypothesis that lies behind the present paper is that the semantics of a language can be regarded as a series of systems of constitutive rules and that illocutionary acts are acts performed in accordance with these sets of constitutive rules. One of the aims of this paper is to formulate a set of constitutive rules for a certain kind of speech act. And if what I have said concerning constitutive rules is correct, we should not be surprised if not all these rules take the form of imperative rules. Indeed we shall see that the rules fall into several different categories, none of which is quite like the rules of etiquette. The effort to state the rules for an illocutionary act can also be regarded as a kind of test of the hypothesis that there are constitutive rules underlying speech acts. If we are unable to give any satisfactory rule formulations, our failure could be construed as partially disconfirming evidence against the hypothesis.

III. PROPOSITIONS

Different illocutionary acts often have features in common with each other. Consider utterances of the following sentences:

(1) Will John leave the room?
(2) John will leave the room.
(3) John, leave the room!
(4) Would that John left the room.
(5) If John will leave the room, I will leave also.

Utterances of each of these on a given occasion would characteristically be performances of different illocutionary acts. The first would, characteristically, be a question, the second an assertion about the future, that is, a prediction, the third a request or

[3] The formulation 'X counts as Y' was originally suggested to me by Max Black.

order, the fourth an expression of a wish, and the fifth a hypothetical expression of intention. Yet in the performance of each the speaker would characteristically perform some subsidiary acts which are common to all five illocutionary acts. In the utterance of each the speaker *refers* to a particular person John and *predicates* the act of leaving the room of that person. In no case is that all he does, but in every case it is a part of what he does. I shall say, therefore, that in each of these cases, although the illocutionary acts are different, at least some of the non-illocutionary acts of reference and predication are the same.

The reference to some person John and predication of the same thing of him in each of these illocutionary acts inclines me to say that there is a common *content* in each of them. Something expressible by the clause 'that John will leave the room' seems to be a common feature of all. We could, with not too much distortion, write each of these sentences in a way which would isolate this common feature: 'I assert that John will leave the room', 'I ask whether John will leave the room', etc.

For lack of a better word I propose to call this common content a proposition, and I shall describe this feature of these illocutionary acts by saying that in the utterance of each of (1)–(5) the speaker expresses the proposition that John will leave the room. Notice that I do not say that the sentence expresses the proposition; I do not know how sentences could perform acts of that kind. But I shall say that in the utterance of the sentence the speaker expresses a proposition. Notice also that I am distinguishing between a proposition and an assertion or statement of that proposition. The proposition that John will leave the room is expressed in the utterance of all of (1)–(5) but only in (2) is that proposition asserted. An assertion is an illocutionary act, but a proposition is not an act at all, although the act of expressing a proposition is a part of performing certain illocutionary acts.

I might summarize this by saying that I am distinguishing between the illocutionary act and the propositional content of an illocutionary act. Of course, not all illocutionary acts have a propositional content, for example, an utterance of 'Hurrah!' or 'Ouch!' does not. In one version or another this distinction is an old one and has been marked in different ways by authors as diverse as Frege, Sheffer, Lewis, Reichenbach and Hare, to mention only a few.

From a semantical point of view we can distinguish between the propositional indicator in the sentence and the indicator of illocutionary force. That is, for a large class of sentences used to perform illocutionary acts, we can say for the purpose of our analysis that the sentence has two (not necessarily separate) parts, the proposition-indicating element and the function-indicating device.[4] The function-indicating device shows how the proposition is to be taken, or, to put it in another way, what illocutionary force the utterance is to have, that is, what illocutionary act the speaker

---

[4] In the sentence 'I promise that I will come' the function-indicating device and the propositional element are separate. In the sentence 'I promise to come', which means the same as the first and is derived from it by certain transformations, the two elements are not separate.

is performing in the utterance of the sentence. Function-indicating devices in English include word order, stress, intonation contour, punctuation, the mood of the verb, and finally a set of so-called performative verbs: I may indicate the kind of illocutionary act I am performing by beginning the sentence with 'I apologize', 'I warn', 'I state', etc. Often in actual speech situations the context will make it clear what the illocutionary force of the utterance is, without its being necessary to invoke the appropriate function indicating device.

If this semantical distinction is of any real importance, it seems likely that it should have some syntactical analogue, and certain recent developments in transformational grammar tend to support the view that it does. In the underlying phrase marker of a sentence there is a distinction between those elements which correspond to the function-indicating device and those which correspond to the propositional content.

The distinction between the function-indicating device and the proposition-indicating device will prove very useful to us in giving an analysis of an illocutionary act. Since the same proposition can be common to all sorts of illocutionary acts, we can separate our analysis of the proposition from our analysis of kinds of illocutionary acts. I think there are rules for expressing propositions, rules for such things as reference and prediction, but those rules can be discussed independently of the rules for function indicating. In this paper I shall not attempt to discuss propositional rules but shall concentrate on rules for using certain kinds of function-indicating devices.

IV. MEANING

Speech acts are characteristically performed in the utterance of sounds or the making of marks. What is the difference between *just* uttering sounds or making marks and performing a speech act? One difference is that the sounds or marks one makes in the performance of a speech act are characteristically said to *have meaning*, and a second related difference is that one is characteristically said to *mean something* by those sounds or marks. Characteristically when one speaks one means something by what one says, and what one says, the string of morphemes that one emits, is characteristically said to have a meaning. Here, incidentally, is another point at which our analogy between performing speech acts and playing games breaks down. The pieces in a game like chess are not characteristically said to have a meaning, and furthermore when one makes a move one is not characteristically said to mean anything by that move.

But what is it for one to mean something by what one says, and what is it for something to have a meaning? To answer the first of these questions I propose to borrow and revise some ideas of Paul Grice. In an article entitled 'Meaning',[5] Grice gives the following analysis of one sense of the notion of 'meaning'. To say that *A* meant something by *x* is to say that '*A* intended the utterance of *x* to produce some

[5] *Philosophical Review*, 1957.

effect in an audience by means of the recognition of this intention'. This seems to me a useful start on an analysis of meaning, first because it shows the close relationship between the notion of meaning and the notion of intention, and secondly because it captures something which is, I think, essential to speaking a language: In speaking a language I attempt to communicate things to my hearer by means of getting him to recognize my intention to communicate just those things. For example, characteristically, when I make an assertion, I attempt to communicate to and convince my hearer of the truth of a certain proposition; and the means I employ to do this are to utter certain sounds, which utterance I intend to produce in him the desired effect by means of his recognition of my intention to produce just that effect. I shall illustrate this with an example. I might on the one hand attempt to get you to believe that I am French by speaking French all the time, dressing in the French manner, showing wild enthusiasm for de Gaulle, and cultivating French acquaintances. But I might on the other hand attempt to get you to believe that I am French by simply telling you that I am French. Now, what is the difference between these two ways of my attempting to get you to believe that I am French? One crucial difference is that in the second case I attempt to get you to believe that I am French by getting you to recognize that it is my purported intention to get you to believe just that. That is one of the things involved in telling you that I am French. But of course if I try to get you to believe that I am French by putting on the act I described, then your recognition of my intention to produce in you the belief that I am French is not the means I am employing. Indeed in this case you would, I think, become rather suspicious if you recognized my intention.

However valuable this analysis of meaning is, it seems to me to be in certain respects defective. First of all, it fails to distinguish the different kinds of effects—perlocutionary versus illocutionary—that one may intend to produce in one's hearers, and it further fails to show the way in which these different kinds of effects are related to the notion of meaning. A second defect is that it fails to account for the extent to which meaning is a matter of rules or conventions. That is, this account of meaning does not show the connection between one's meaning something by what one says and what that which one says actually means in the language. In order to illustrate this point I now wish to present a counter-example to this analysis of meaning. The point of the counter-example will be to illustrate the connection between what a speaker means and what the words he utters mean.

Suppose that I am an American soldier in the Second World War and that I am captured by Italian troops. And suppose also that I wish to get these troops to believe that I am a German officer in order to get them to release me. What I would like to do is to tell them in German or Italian that I am a German officer. But let us suppose I don't know enough German or Italian to do that. So I, as it were, attempt to put on a show of telling them that I am a German officer by reciting those few bits of German that I know, trusting that they don't know enough German to see through my plan. Let us suppose I know only one line of German, which I remember from a poem I had to memorize in a high-school German course. Therefore I, a captured American, address my Italian captors with the following sentence: 'Kennst du das Land, wo die Zitronen blühen?' Now, let us describe the situation in Gricean terms. I intend to produce a certain effect in them, namely, the effect of believing that I am a German officer; and I intend to produce this effect by means of their recognition of my intention. I intend that they should think that what I am trying to tell them is that I am a German officer. But does it follow from this account that when I say 'Kennst du das Land . . .' etc., what I mean is, 'I am a German officer'? Not only does it not follow, but in this case it seems plainly false that when I utter the German sentence what I mean is 'I am a German officer', or even 'Ich bin ein deutscher Offizier', because what the words mean is, 'Knowest thou the land where the lemon trees bloom?' Of course, I want my captors to be deceived into thinking that what I mean is 'I am a German officer', but part of what is involved in the deception is getting them to think that that is what the words which I utter mean in German. At one point in the *Philosophical Investigations* Wittgenstein says 'Say "it's cold here" and mean "it's warm here"'.[6] The reason we are unable to do this is that what we can mean is a function of what we are saying. Meaning is more than a matter of intention, it is also a matter of convention.

Grice's account can be amended to deal with counter-examples of this kind. We have here a case where I am trying to produce a certain effect by means of the recognition of my intention to produce that effect, but the device I use to produce this effect is one which is conventionally, by the rules governing the use of that device, used as a means of producing quite different illocutionary effects. We must therefore reformulate the Gricean account of meaning in such a way as to make it clear that one's meaning something when one says something is more than just contingently related to what the sentence means in the language one is speaking. In our analysis of illocutionary acts, we must capture both the intentional and the conventional aspects and especially the relationship between them. In the performance of an illocutionary act the speaker intends to produce a certain effect by means of getting the hearer to recognize his intention to produce that effect, and furthermore, if he is using words literally, he intends this recognition to be achieved in virtue of the fact that the rules for using the expressions he utters associate the expressions with the production of that effect. It is this *combination* of elements which we shall need to express in our analysis of the illocutionary act.

V. HOW TO PROMISE

I shall now attempt to give an analysis of the illocutionary act of promising. In order to do this I shall ask what conditions are necessary and sufficient for the act of

---

[6] *Philosophical Investigations* (Oxford, 1953), para. 510.

promising to have been performed in the utterance of a given sentence. I shall attempt to answer this question by stating these conditions as a set of propositions such that the conjunction of the members of the set entails the proposition that a speaker made a promise, and the proposition that the speaker made a promise entails this conjunction. Thus each condition will be a necessary condition for the performance of the act of promising and taken collectively the set of conditions will be a sufficient condition for the act to have been performed.

If we get such a set of conditions we can extract from them a set of rules for the use of the function-indicating device. The method here is analogous to discovering the rules of chess by asking oneself what are the necessary and sufficient conditions under which one can be said to have correctly moved a knight or castled or check-mated a player, etc. We are in the position of someone who has learned to play chess without ever having the rules formulated and who wants such a formulation. We learned how to play the game of illocutionary acts, but in general it was done without an explicit formulation of the rules, and the first step in getting such a formulation is to set out the conditions for the performance of a particular illocutionary act. Our inquiry will therefore serve a double philosophical purpose. By stating a set of conditions for the performance of a particular illocutionary act we shall have offered a partial explication of that notion and shall also have paved the way for the second step, the formulation of the rules.

I find the statement of the conditions very difficult to do, and I am not entirely satisfied with the list I am about to present. One reason for the difficulty is that the notion of a promise, like most notions in ordinary language, does not have absolutely strict rules. There are all sorts of odd, deviant, and borderline promises; and counter-examples, more or less bizarre, can be produced against my analysis. I am inclined to think we shall not be able to get a set of knock-down necessary and sufficient conditions that will exactly mirror the ordinary use of the word 'promise'. I am confining my discussion, therefore, to the centre of the concept of promising and ignoring the fringe, borderline, and partially defective cases. I also confine my discussion to full-blown explicit promises and ignore promises made by elliptical turns of phrase, hints, metaphors, etc.

Another difficulty arises from my desire to state the conditions without certain forms of circularity. I want to give a list of conditions for the performance of a certain illocutionary act, which do not themselves mention the performance of any illocutionary acts. I need to satisfy this condition in order to offer an explication of the notion of an illocutionary act in general, otherwise I should simply be showing the relation between different illocutionary acts. However, although there will be no reference to illocutionary *acts*, certain illocutionary *concepts* will appear in the analysans as well as in the analysandum; and I think this form of circularity is unavoidable because of the nature of constitutive rules.

In the presentation of the conditions I shall first consider the case of a sincere promise and then show how to modify the conditions to allow for insincere promises. As our inquiry is semantical rather than syntactical, I shall simply assume the existence of grammatically well-formed sentences.

Given that a speaker *S* utters a sentence *T* in the presence of a hearer *H*, then, in the utterance of *T*, *S* sincerely (and non-defectively) promises that *p* to *H* if and only if:

(1) *Normal input and output conditions obtain.*

I use the terms 'input' and 'output' to cover the large and indefinite range of conditions under which any kind of serious linguistic communication is possible. 'Output' covers the conditions for intelligible speaking and 'input' covers the conditions for understanding. Together they include such things as that the speaker and hearer both know how to speak the language; both are conscious of what they are doing; the speaker is not acting under duress or threats; they have no physical impediments to communication, such as deafness, aphasia, or laryngitis; they are not acting in a play or telling jokes, etc.

(2) *S expresses that p in the utterance of T.*

This condition isolates the propositional content from the rest of the speech act and enables us to concentrate on the peculiarities of promising in the rest of the analysis.

(3) *In expressing that p, S predicates a future act A of S.*

In the case of promising the function-indicating device is an expression whose scope includes certain features of the proposition. In a promise an act must be predicated of the speaker and it cannot be a past act. I cannot promise to have done something, and I cannot promise that someone else will do something. (Although I can promise to see that he will do it.) The notion of an act, as I am construing it for present purposes, includes refraining from acts, performing series of acts, and may also include states and conditions: I may promise not to do something, I may promise to do something repeatedly, and I may promise to be or remain in a certain state or condition. I call conditions (2) and (3) the *propositional content conditions.*

(4) *H would prefer S's doing A to his not doing A, and S believes H would prefer his doing A to his not doing A.*

One crucial distinction between promises on the one hand and threats on the other is that a promise is a pledge to do something for you, not to you, but a threat is a pledge to do something to you, not for you. A promise is defective if the thing promised is something the promisee does not want done; and it is further defective if the promisor does not believe the promisee wants it done, since a non-defective promise must be intended as a promise and not as a threat or warning. I think both halves of this double condition are necessary in order to avoid fairly obvious counter-examples.

One can, however, think of apparent counter-examples to this condition as stated.

Suppose I say to a lazy student 'If you don't hand in your paper on time I promise you I will give you a failing grade in the course'. Is this utterance a promise? I am inclined to think not; we would more naturally describe it as a warning or possibly even a threat. But why then is it possible to use the locution 'I promise' in such a case? I think we use it here because 'I promise' and 'I hereby promise' are among the strongest function-indicating devices for *commitment* provided by the English language. For that reason we often use these expressions in the performance of speech acts which are not strictly speaking promises but in which we wish to emphasize our commitment. To illustrate this, consider another apparent counter-example to the analysis along different lines. Sometimes, more commonly I think in the United States than in England, one hears people say 'I promise' when making an emphatic assertion. Suppose, for example, I accuse you of having stolen the money. I say, 'You stole that money, didn't you?' You reply 'No, I didn't, I promise you I didn't'. Did you make a promise in this case? I find it very unnatural to describe your utterance as a promise. This utterance would be more aptly described as an emphatic denial, and we can explain the occurrence of the function-indicating device 'I promise' as derivative from genuine promises and serving here as an expression adding emphasis to your denial.

In general the point stated in condition (4) is that if a purported promise is to be non-defective the thing promised must be something the hearer wants done, or considers to be in his interest, or would prefer being done to not being done, etc.; and the speaker must be aware of or believe or know, etc., that this is the case. I think a more elegant and exact formulation of this condition would require the introduction of technical terminology.

(5) *It is not obvious to both S and H that S will do A in the normal course of events.*

This condition is an instance of a general condition on many different kinds of illocutionary acts to the effect that the act must have a point. For example, if I make a request to someone to do something which it is obvious that he is already doing or is about to do, then my request is pointless and to that extent defective. In an actual speech situation, listeners, knowing the rules for performing illocutionary acts, will assume that this condition is satisfied. Suppose, for example, that in the course of a public speech I say to a member of my audience 'Look here, Smith, pay attention to what I am saying'. In order to make sense of this utterance the audience will have to assume that Smith has not been paying attention or at any rate that it is not obvious that he has been paying attention, that the question of his paying attention has arisen in some way; because a condition for making a request is that it is not obvious that the hearer is doing or about to do the thing requested.

Similarly with promises. It is out of order for me to promise to do something that it is obvious I am going to do anyhow. If I do seem to be making such a promise, the only way my audience can make sense of my utterance is to assume that I believe that it is not obvious that I am going to do the thing promised. A happily married man who promises his wife he will not desert her in the next week is likely to provide more anxiety than comfort.

Parenthetically I think this condition is an instance of the sort of phenomenon stated in Zipf's law. I think there is operating in our language, as in most forms of human behaviour, a principle of least effort, in this case a principle of maximum illocutionary ends with minimum phonetic effort; and I think condition (5) is an instance of it.

I call conditions such as (4) and (5) *preparatory conditions*. They are *sine quibus non* of happy promising, but they do not yet state the essential feature.

(6) *S intends to do A.*

The most important distinction between sincere and insincere promises is that in the case of the insincere promise the speaker intends to do the act promised, in the case of the insincere promise he does not intend to do the act. Also in sincere promises the speaker believes it is possible for him to do the act (or refrain from doing it), but I think the proposition that he intends to do it entails that he thinks it is possible to do (or refrain from doing) it, so I am not stating that as an extra condition. I call this condition the *sincerity condition*.

(7) *S intends that the utterance of T will place him under an obligation to do A.*

The essential feature of a promise is that it is the undertaking of an obligation to perform a certain act. I think that this condition distinguishes promises (and other members of the same family such as vows) from other kinds of speech acts. Notice that in the statement of the condition we only specify the speaker's intention; further conditions will make clear how that intention is realized. It is clear, however, that having this intention is a necessary condition of making a promise; for if a speaker can demonstrate that he did not have this intention in a given utterance, he can prove that the utterance was not a promise. We know, for example, that Mr. Pickwick did not promise to marry the woman because we know he did not have the appropriate intention.

I call this the *essential condition*.

(8) *S intends that the utterance of T will produce in H a belief that conditions (6) and (7) obtain by means of the recognition of the intention to produce that belief, and he intends this recognition to be achieved by means of the recognition of the sentence as one conventionally used to produce such beliefs.*

This captures our amended Gricean analysis of what it is for the speaker to mean to make a promise. The speaker intends to produce a certain illocutionary effect by means of getting the hearer to recognize his intention to produce that effect, and he also intends this recognition to be achieved in virtue of the fact that the lexical and syntactical character of the item he utters conventionally associates it with producing that effect.

Strictly speaking this condition could be formulated as part of condition (1), but it is of enough philosophical interest to be worth stating separately. I find it troublesome for the following reason. If my original objection to Grice is really valid, then surely, one might say, all these iterated intentions are superfluous; all that is necessary is that the speaker should seriously utter a sentence. The production of all these effects is simply a consequence of the hearer's knowledge of what the sentence means, which in turn is a consequence of his knowledge of the language, which is assumed by the speaker at the outset. I think the correct reply to this objection is that condition (8) explicates what it is for the speaker to 'seriously' utter the sentence, i.e. to utter it and mean it, but I am not completely confident about either the force of the objection or of the reply.

(9) *The semantical rules of the dialect spoken by S and H are such that T is correctly and sincerely uttered if and only if conditions (1)–(8) obtain.*

This condition is intended to make clear that the sentence uttered is one which by the semantical rules of the language is used to make a promise. Taken together with condition (8), it eliminates counter-examples like the captured soldier example considered earlier. Exactly what the formulation of the rules is, we shall soon see.

So far we have considered only the case of a sincere promise. But insincere promises are promises none the less, and we now need to show how to modify the conditions to allow for them. In making an insincere promise the speaker does not have all the intentions and beliefs he has when making a sincere promise. However, he purports to have them. Indeed it is because he purports to have intentions and beliefs which he does not have that we describe his act as insincere. So to allow for insincere promises we need only to revise our conditions to state that the speaker takes responsibility for having the beliefs and intentions rather than stating that he actually has them. A clue that the speaker does take such responsibility is the fact that he could not say without absurdity, e.g., 'I promise to do *A* but I do not intend to do *A*'. To say 'I promise to do *A*' is to take responsibility for intending to do *A*, and this condition holds whether the utterance was sincere or insincere. To allow for the possibility of an insincere promise then we have only to revise condition (6) so that it states not that the speaker intends to do *A*, but that he takes responsibility for intending to do *A*, and to avoid the charge of circularity I shall phrase this as follows:

(6*) *S intends that the utterance of T will make him responsible for intending to do A.*

Thus amended (and with 'sincerely' dropped from our analysandum and from condition (9)), our analysis is neutral on the question whether the promise was sincere or insincere.

VI. RULES FOR THE USE OF THE FUNCTION-INDICATING DEVICE

Our next task is to extract from our set of conditions a set of rules for the use of the function-indicating device. Obviously not all of our conditions are equally relevant to this task. Condition (1) and conditions of the forms (8) and (9) apply generally to all kinds of normal illocutionary acts and are not peculiar to promising. Rules for the function-indicating device for promising are to be found corresponding to conditions (2)–(7).

The semantic rules for the use of any function-indicating device P for promising are:

Rule 1. P is to be uttered only in the context of a sentence (or larger stretch of discourse) the utterance of which predicates some future act A of the speaker S.
I call this the *propositional-content rule*. It is derived from the propositional-content conditions (2) and (3).

Rule 2. P is to be utterred only if the hearer H would prefer S's doing A to his not doing A, and S believes H would prefer S's doing A to his not doing A.

Rule 3. P is to be uttered only if it is not obvious to both S and H that S will do A in the normal course of events.
I call rules (2) and (3) *preparatory rules*. They are derived from the preparatory conditions (4) and (5).

Rule 4. P is to be uttered only if S intends to do A.
I call this the *sincerity rule*. It is derived from the sincerity condition (6).

Rule 5. The utterance of P counts as the undertaking of an obligation to do A.
I call this the *essential rule*.

These rules are ordered: rules 2–5 apply only if rule 1 is satisfied, and rule 5 applies only if rules 2 and 3 are satisfied as well.

Notice that whereas rules 1–4 take the form of quasi-imperatives, i.e. they are of the form: utter P only if x, rule 5 is of the form: the utterance of P counts as Y. Thus rule 5 is of the kind peculiar to systems of constitutive rules which I discussed in section II.

Notice also that the rather tiresome analogy with games is holding up remarkably well. If we ask ourselves under what conditions a player could be said to move a knight correctly, we would find preparatory conditions, such as that it must be his turn to move, as well as the essential condition stating the actual positions the knight can move to. I think that there is even a sincerity rule for competitive games, the rule that each side tries to win. I suggest that the team which 'throws' the game is behaving in a way closely analogous to the speaker who lies or makes false promises. Of course, there usually are no propositional-content rules for games, because games do not, by and large, represent states of affairs.

If this analysis is of any general interest beyond the case of promising then it would seem that these distinctions should carry over into other types of speech act, and I think a little reflection will show that they do. Consider, e.g., giving an order. The preparatory conditions include that the speaker should be in a position of authority over the hearer, the sincerity condition is that the speaker wants the ordered act done, and the essential condition has to do with the fact that the utterance is an attempt to get the hearer to do it. For assertions, the preparatory conditions include the fact that the hearer must have some basis for supposing the asserted proposition is true, the sincerity condition is that he must believe it to be true, and the essential condition has to do with the fact that the utterance is an attempt to inform the hearer and convince him of its truth. Greetings are a much simpler kind of speech act, but even here some of the distinctions apply. In the utterance of 'Hello' there is no propositional content and no sincerity condition. The preparatory conditon is that the speaker must have just encountered the hearer, and the essential rule is that the utterance indicates courteous recognition of the hearer.

A proposal for further research then is to carry out a similar analysis of other types of speech acts. Not only would this give us an analysis of concepts interesting in themselves, but the comparison of different analyses would deepen our understanding of the whole subject and incidentally provide a basis for a more serious taxonomy than any of the usual facile categories such as evaluative versus descriptive, or cognitive versus emotive.

IV

UTTERER'S MEANING, SENTENCE-MEANING, AND WORD-MEANING[1]

H. P. GRICE

A. PROLEGOMENA

My aim in this paper is to throw light on the connection between (a) a notion of meaning which I want to regard as basic, viz. that notion which is involved in saying of someone that by (when) doing such-and-such he meant that so-and-so (in what I have called a non-natural sense of the word 'meant'), and (b) the notions of meaning involved in saying (i) that a given sentence means 'so-and-so' (ii) that a given word or phrase means 'so-and-so'. What I have to say on these topics should be looked upon as an attempt to provide a sketch of what might, I hope, prove to be a viable theory, rather than as an attempt to provide any part of a finally acceptable theory. The account which I shall offer of the (for me) basic notion of meaning is one which I shall not today seek to defend; I should like its approximate correctness to be assumed, so that attention may be focused on its utility, if correct, in the explication of other and (I hope) derivative notions of meaning. This enterprise forms part of a wider programme which I shall in a moment delineate, though its later stages lie beyond the limits which I have set for this paper.

The wider programme just mentioned arises out of a distinction which, for purposes which I need not here specify, I wish to make within the total signification of a remark: a distinction between what the speaker has *said* (in a certain favoured, and maybe in some degree artificial, sense of 'said'), and what he has 'implicated' (e.g. implied, indicated, suggested, etc.), taking into account the fact that what he has implicated may be either *conventionally* implicated (implicated by virtue of the meaning of some word or phrase which he has used) or *non-conventionally* implicated (in which case the specification of the implicature falls outside the specification of the conventional meaning of the words used). The programme is directed towards an explication of the favoured sense of 'say' and a clarification of its relation to the notion of conventional meaning.

The stages of the programme are as follows:

(I) To distinguish between locutions of the form 'U (utterer) meant *that* ...' (locutions which specify what might be called 'occasion-meaning') and locutions of the

From *Foundations of Language*, 4 (1968), pp. 1–18. Reprinted by permission of the author and the editor of *Foundations of Language*.

[1] I hope that material in this paper, revised and re-arranged, will form part of a book to be published by the Harvard University Press.

form 'X (utterance-type) means "…"'. In locutions of the first type, meaning is specified without the use of quotation-marks, whereas in locutions of the second type the meaning of a sentence, word or phrase is specified with the aid of quotation-marks. This difference is semantically important.

(II) To attempt to provide a definiens for statements of occasion-meaning; more precisely, to provide a definiens for 'By (when) uttering x, U meant that ∗p'. Some explanatory comments are needed here.

(a) I use the term 'utter' (together with 'utterance') in an artificially wide sense, to cover any case of doing x or producing x by the performance of which U meant that so-and-so. The performance in question need not be a linguistic or even a conventionalized performance. A specificatory replacement of the dummy 'x' will in some cases be a characterization of a deed, in others a characterization of a product (e.g. a sound).

(b) '∗' is a *dummy* mood-indicator, distinct from specific mood-indicators like '⊢' (indicative or assertive) or '!' (imperative). More precisely, one may think of the schema 'Jones meant that ∗p' as yielding a full English sentence after two transformational steps:

(i) replace '∗' by a specific mood-indicator and replace 'p' by an indicative sentence. One might thus get to

'Jones meant that ⊢ Smith will go home'

or to   'Jones meant that ! Smith will go home'.

(ii) replace the sequence following the word 'that' by an appropriate clause in indirect speech (in accordance with rules specified in a linguistic theory). One might thus get to

'Jones meant that Smith will go home'

'Jones meant that Smith is to go home'.

(III) To attempt to elucidate the notion of the conventional meaning of an utterance-type; more precisely, to explicate sentences which make claims of the form 'X (utterance-type) means "∗"', or, in case X is a non-sentential utterance-type, claims of the form 'X means "…"', where the location is completed by a non-sentential expression. Again, some explanatory comments are required.

(a) It will be convenient to recognize that what I shall call statements of *timeless meaning* (statements of the type 'X means "…"', in which the specification of meaning involves quotation-marks) may be subdivided into (i) statements of timeless 'idiolect-meaning', e.g. 'For U (in U's idiolect) X means "…"' and (ii) statements of timeless 'language meaning', e.g. 'In L (language) X means "…"'. It will be convenient to handle these separately, and in the order just given.

(b) The truth of a statement to the effect that X means '…' is of course not incompatible with the truth of a further statement to the effect that X means '—', when the two lacunae are quite differently completed. An utterance-type may have more than one conventional meaning, and any definiens which we offer must allow for this fact. 'X means "…" ' should be understood as 'One of the meanings of X is "…" '.

(IV) In view of the possibility of multiplicity in the timeless meaning of an utterance-type, we shall need to notice, and to provide an explication of, what I shall call the *applied timeless meaning* of an utterance-type. That is to say, we need a definiens for the schema 'X (utterance-type) meant *here* "…" ', a schema the specifications of which announce the correct reading of X for a given occasion of utterance.

Comments. (a) We must be careful to distinguish the applied timeless meaning of X (type) with respect to a particular token x (belonging to X) from the occasion-meaning of U's utterance of x. The following are not equivalent:

(i) 'When U uttered it, the sentence "Palmer gave Nicklaus quite a beating" meant "Palmer vanquished Nicklaus with some ease" [rather than, say, "Palmer administered vigorous corporal punishment to Nicklaus."]'

(ii) 'When U uttered the sentence "Palmer gave Nicklaus quite a beating" U meant that Palmer vanquished Nicklaus with some ease.'

U might have been speaking ironically, in which case he would very likely have meant that *Nicklaus* vanquished *Palmer* with some ease. In that case (ii) would clearly be false; but nevertheless (i) would still have been true.

(b) There is some temptation to take the view that the conjunction of

(i) 'By uttering X, U meant that *p' and

(ii) 'When uttered by U, X meant "*p" '

provides a definiens for 'In uttering X, U said that *p'. Indeed, if we give consideration only to utterance-types for which there are available adequate statements of timeless meaning taking the exemplary form 'X meant "*p" ' (or, in the case of applied timeless meaning, the form 'X meant here "*p" '), it may even be possible to uphold the thesis that such a coincidence of occasion-meaning and applied timeless meaning is a necessary and sufficient condition for saying that *p. But a little reflection should convince us of the need to recognize the existence of statements of timeless meaning which instantiate forms other than the cited exemplary form; there are, I think, at least some sentences whose timeless meaning is not adequately specifiable by a statement of the exemplary form. Consider the sentence 'Bill is a philosopher and he is, therefore, brave' (S_1). It would be appropriate, I think, to make a partial specification of the timeless meaning of S_1 by saying 'Part of one meaning of S_1 is "Bill is occupationally engaged in philosophical studies" '. One might, indeed, give a full specification of timeless meaning for S_1 by saying 'One meaning of S_1 includes "Bill is occupationally engaged in philosophical studies" and "Bill is courageous" and "That Bill is courageous follows from his being occupationally engaged in philosophical studies", and that is all that is included'. [We might re-express this as 'One meaning of S_1 *comprises* "Bill is occupationally engaged (etc)", "Bill is courageous", and "That Bill is courageous follows (etc.)".'] It will be preferable to specify the timeless meaning of S_1 in this way than to do so as follows: 'One meaning of S_1 is "Bill is occupationally engaged (etc.) and Bill is courageous and that Bill is courageous follows (etc.)"'; for this latter formulation at least suggests that S_1 is synonymous with the conjunctive sentence quoted in the formulation, which does not seem to be the case.

Since it is true that *another* meaning of S_1 includes 'Bill is addicted to general reflections about life' (*vice* 'Bill is occupationally engaged (etc.)'), one could have occasion to say (truly), with respect to a given utterance by U of S_1, 'The meaning of S_1 *here* comprised "Bill is occupationally engaged (etc.)", "Bill is courageous", and "That Bill is courageous follows (etc.)"', or to say 'The meaning of S_1 *here* included "That Bill is courageous follows (etc.)"'. It could also be true that when U uttered S_1 he meant (part of what he meant was) *that* that Bill is courageous follows (etc.).

Now I do not wish to allow that, in my favoured sense of 'say', one who utters S_1 will have *said* that Bill's being courageous follows from his being a philosopher, though he may well have said that Bill is a philosopher and that Bill is courageous. I would wish to maintain that the semantic function of the word 'therefore' is to enable a speaker to *indicate*, though not to *say*, that a certain consequence holds. *Mutatis mutandis*, I would adopt the same position with regard to words like 'but' and 'moreover'. My primary reason for opting for this particular sense of 'say' is that I expect it to be of greater theoretical utility than some other sense of 'say' would be. So I shall be committed to the view that applied timeless meaning and occasion-meaning may coincide, that is to say, it may be true both (i) that when U uttered X the meaning of X included '$*p$' and (ii) that part of what U meant when he uttered X was that $*p$, and yet be false that U has said, among other things, that $*p$. I would like to use the expression 'conventionally meant that' in such a way that the fulfilment of the two conditions just mentioned, while insufficient for the truth of 'U said that $*p$' will be sufficient (and necessary) for the truth of 'U conventionally meant that $*p$'.

(V) This distinction between what is said and what is conventionally meant creates the task of specifying the conditions in which what U conventionally meant by an utterance is also part of what U said. I have hopes of being able to discharge this task by proceeding along the following lines:

(1) To specify conditions which will be satisfied only by a limited range of speech-acts, the members of which will thereby be stamped as specially central or fundamental.

(2) To stipulate that in uttering X, U will have said that $*p$, if both (i) U has Y-ed that $*p$, where Y-ing is a central speech-act, and (ii) X embodies some conventional device the meaning of which is such that its presence in X indicates that its utterer is Y-ing that $*p$.

(3) To define, for each member Y of the range of central speech-acts, 'U has Y-ed

that ∗p' in terms of occasion-meaning (meaning that...) or in terms of some important element(s) involved in the already provided definition of occasion-meaning.

(VI) The fulfilment of the task just outlined will need to be supplemented by an account of the elements in the conventional meaning of an utterance which are *not* part of what has been said. This account, at least for an important sub-class of such elements, might take the following shape:

(1) The problematic elements are linked with certain speech-acts which are exhibited as posterior to, and such that their performance is dependent upon, some member or disjunction of members of the central range; for example, the meaning of 'moreover' would be linked with the speech-act of adding, the performance of which would require the performance of one or other of the central speech-acts.

(2) If Z-ing is such a non-central speech-act, the dependence of Z-ing that ∗p upon the performance of some central speech-act would have to be shown to be of a nature which justifies a reluctance to treat Z-ing that ∗p as a case not merely of saying that ∗p, but also of saying that = p, or of saying that = ∗p (where ' = p', or ' = ∗p', is a representation of one or more sentential forms specifically associated with Z-ing).[2]

(3) The notion of Z-ing that ∗p (where Z-ing is non-central) would be explicated in terms of the notion of *meaning that* (or in terms of some important element(s) in the definition of that notion).

B. TREATMENT OF SOME OF THE PROBLEMS RAISED

The problems which I shall consider in the remainder of this paper are those which are presented by Stages II–IV of the programme just outlined.

Stage II   I shall offer, without arguing for it, a somewhat over-simplified account of the notion of occasion-meaning, which (as I said at the outset) I should like to be treated as if it were correct.

In my 1957 article on 'Meaning'[3] I in effect suggested, for the schema 'U meant (non-naturally) something by uttering x', a three-clause definiens which may be compendiously reformulated as 'For some audience A, U intended his utterance of x to produce in A some effect (response) E, by means of A's recognition of that intention'. As I wish to continue to use the central idea of this definition, I shall introduce an abbreviation; 'U intends to produce in A effect E by means of A's recognition of that intention' will be abbreviated to 'U *M-intends* to produce in A effect E'. ('M' for 'meaning'.)

The point of divergence between my current account and my 1957 account lies in the characterization of the M-intended effect (response). In the earlier account I took the view that the M-intended effect is, in the case of indicative-type utterances, that the

---

[2] As 'moreover ____' is specifically associated with the speech-act of adding.

[3] [*Philosophical Review*, LXVII (1957).]

hearer should *believe* something, and, in the case of imperative-type utterances, that the hearer should *do* something. I wish for present purposes to make two changes here.

(1) I wish to represent the M-intended effect of imperative-type utterances as being that the hearer should *intend* to do something (with, of course, the ulterior intention on the part of the utterer that the hearer should go on to do the act in question).

(2) I wish to regard the M-intended effect common to indicative-type utterances as being, not that the hearer should believe something (though there will frequently be an ulterior intention to that effect), but that the hearer should *think that the utterer believes* something.

The effect of the first change will be that the way is opened to a simplified treatment of the M-intended effect, as being always the generation of some propositional attitude. The effect of the second change (made in order to unify the treatment of indicative-type utterances, some of which are, and some of which are not, cases of informing or telling) will be to introduce a distinction between what I might call *exhibitive* utterances (utterances by which the utterer U M-intends to impart a belief that he (U) has a certain propositional attitude) and utterances which are not only exhibitive but also what I might call *protreptic* (utterances by which U M-intends, *via* imparting a belief that he (U) has a certain propositional attitude, to induce a corresponding attitude in the hearer).

I shall now try to reformulate the account in a generalized form. Let 'A' range over audiences or hearers. Let the device '$*\psi$' (read 'asterisk-sub-ψ') be a dummy, which represents a specific mood-indicator which corresponds to the propositional attitude ψ-ing (whichever that may be), as for example, '⊢' corresponds to believing (thinking) and '!' corresponds to intending. I can, using this device, offer the following rough definition:

D.1. 'By (when) uttering x U meant that $*\psi$p' = df. '($\exists$A) (U uttered x M-intending (i) that A should think U to ψ that p and in some cases only [depending on the identification of "$*\psi$p "], (ii) that A should, via the fulfilment of (i), himself ψ that p)'.

It will be convenient to have an abbreviated version of this definiens. Let the device 'ψ^+' (read 'ψ-dagger') be a dummy which operates as follows: in some cases the phrase 'that A should ψ^+ that p' is to be interpreted as 'that A should think U to ψ that p'; in other cases this phrase is to be interpreted as 'that A should ψ that p (via thinking U to ψ that p)'. Which interpretation is to be selected is determined by the specification of '$*\psi$p'. We may now reformulate D.1 as follows:

D.1'. 'By (when) uttering x U meant that $*\psi$p' = df. '($\exists$A) (U uttered x M-intending that A should ψ^+ that p)'.

To meet all the difficulties to which my 1957 account (which was only intended as a model) is exposed, a very much more complicated definition is required. But as the examples which force the introduction of this complexity involve relatively sophisticated kinds of communication or linguistic performance, I hope that, for working purposes, the proffered definition will be adequate.

Stage III   (Step (1): timeless meaning for unstructured utterance-types)

It is, I think, extremely important to distinguish two problems.

(1) What is the relation between timeless meaning (for complete utterance-types) and occasion-meaning?

(2) In the case of syntactically structured (linguistic) utterance-types, how is the timeless meaning of a complete (sentential) utterance-type related to the timeless meanings of its non-complete structured and unstructured elements (approximately, phrases and words), and what account is to be given of timeless meaning for non-complete utterance-types?

If we do not treat these problems separately, we shall have only ourselves to blame for the confusion in which we shall find ourselves. So initially I shall restrict myself to examining the notion of timeless meaning in its application to unstructured utterance-types. My main example will be a gesture (a signal), and it will be convenient first to consider the idea of its timeless meaning for an individual (within a signalling idiolect, so to speak); and only afterwards to consider the extension of this idea to groups of individuals. We shall thus preserve for the time being the possibility of keeping distinct the ideas of having an *established* meaning and of having a *conventional* meaning.

Suppose that a particular sort of hand-wave (to be referred to as H-W) for a particular individual U (within U's idiolect) means 'I know the route'. We are to look for an explication of the sentence 'For U, H-W means "I know the route" ' which will relate timeless meaning to occasion-meaning. As a first shot one might suggest something like 'It is U's policy (practice, habit) to utter H-W in order to *mean that* U knows the route' (where 'mean that' is to be analysed in accordance with D.1.); or, more perspicuously, 'It is U's policy (practice, habit) to utter H-W iff U is making an utterance by which U *means that* U knows the route'.

If we apply D.1. to this suggested definiens, we shall get the following expanded definiens: 'It is U's policy (practice, habit) to utter H-W iff U is making an utterance by means of which (for some A) U M-intends to effect that A thinks U to think that U knows the route'. Now, whether or not this definiens is otherwise acceptable, I wish to argue that the notion of M-intention is otiose here, and that only the notion of simple intention need be invoked; if U's policy (practice, habit) is such that his use of H-W is tied to the presence of a *simple* intention to affect an audience in the way described, it will follow that when, on a given occasion, he utters H-W, he will do so, on that occasion, M-intending to affect his audience in that way.

Suppose that, using only the notion of simple intention, we specify U's policy as follows: 'I (that is, utterer U) shall utter H-W iff I intend (want) some A to think that I think I know the route'. Now, if U is ever to have the particular intentions which will be involved in every implementation of this policy, he must (logically) be in a position, when uttering H-W, to suppose that there is at least some chance that these intentions will be realized; for such a supposition to be justified, as U well knows, a given audience A must be aware of U's policy and must suppose it to apply to the utterance of H-W with which U has presented him. U, then, when uttering H-W on a particular occasion, must expect A to think (or at least to be in a position to think) as follows: 'U's policy for H-W is such that he utters H-W now with the intention that I should think that he thinks that he knows the route; in that case, I take it that he does think that he knows the route'. But to utter H-W expecting A to respond in such a way *is* to utter H-W M-intending that A should think that U thinks that U knows the route. So a formulation of U's policy of H-W in terms of the notion of simple intention is adequate to ensure that, by a particular utterance of H-W, U will *mean that* he knows the route.

We may, then, suggest a simplified definition: 'For U, H-W means "I know the route"' = df. 'It is U's policy (practice, habit) to utter H-W iff, for some A, U intends (wants) A to think that U thinks U knows the route'. This definition, however, is doubly unacceptable. (1) For U, H-W may have a second meaning; it may also mean 'I am about to leave you'. If that is so, U's policy (etc.) cannot be to utter H-W *only if* U wants some A to think that U thinks U knows the route; sometimes he will be ready to utter H-W wanting some A to think that U thinks that U is about to leave A. (2) U may have other ways of getting an A to think that U thinks that U knows the route (such as saying 'I know the route'), and may be ready, on occasion, to employ them. That being so, U's policy (etc.) cannot be to utter H-W *if* (i.e. whenever) U wants an A to think that U thinks U knows the route.

To cope with these difficulties, I think I need some such idea as that of 'having a certain procedure in one's repertoire'. This idea seems to me to be intuitively fairly intelligible and to have application outside the realm of linguistic, or otherwise communicative, performances, though it could hardly be denied that it requires further explication. A faintly eccentric lecturer might have in his repertoire the following procedure: if he sees an attractive girl in his audience, to pause for half a minute and then take a sedative. His having in his repertoire this procedure would not be incompatible with his also having two further procedures: (a) if he sees an attractive girl, to put on a pair of dark spectacles (instead of pausing and taking a sedative); (b) to pause and take a sedative when he sees in his audience not an attractive girl, but a particularly distinguished colleague. Somewhat similarly, if U has in his repertoire the procedure of uttering H-W if he wants an audience A to think U thinks U knows the route, this fact would not be incompatible with his having at least two further procedures: (a) to say 'I know the route' if he wants some A to think U thinks U knows the route; and (b) to utter H-W if U wants some A to think U thinks he is about to leave A. So I propose the definition:

D.2. 'For U utterance-type X means (has as one of its meanings) "$*\psi p$"' = df. 'U has in his repertoire the following procedure: to utter a token of X if U intends (wants) A to ψ^+ that p'.

We may now turn from the idea of timeless meaning within an 'idiolect' to that of timeless meaning for a group or class of individuals. If U utters H-W, his measure of expectation of success as regards effecting the intended response obviously depends (as has already been remarked) on A's knowledge of U's procedure; and in general, unless the signal is to be explained to each A, on A's repertoire containing the same procedure. So obviously each member of some group G (within which H-W is to be a tool of communication) will want his procedure with respect to H-W to conform to the general practice of the group. So I suggest the following rough definition:

D.3. 'For group G, utterance-type X means "$*\psi p$"' = df. 'At least some (? many) members of group G have in their repertoires the procedure of uttering a token of X if, for some A, they want A to $\psi^{\dagger}$ that p; the retention of this procedure being for them conditional on the assumption that at least some (other) members of G have, or have had, this procedure in their repertoires'. D.3. gets in the idea of aiming at conformity, and so perhaps (derivatively) also that of *correct* and *incorrect* use of X, as distinct from the idea merely of usual or unusual use of X.

The explication of the notion of 'having a procedure in one's repertoire' is, to my mind, a task of considerable difficulty. I have felt inclined to propose, as a make-shift definition, the following:

'U has in his repertoire the procedure of ...' = df. 'U has a standing readiness (willingness, preparedness), in some degree, to ...', a readiness (etc.) to do something being a member of the same family (a weaker brother, so to speak) as an intention to do that thing. But this definition would clearly be inadequate as it stands; it may well be true that, for my exceedingly prim Aunt Matilda, the expression 'he is a runt' means 'he is an undersized person', and yet quite false that she has *any* degree of readiness to utter the expression in any circumstances whatsoever. What one seems to need is the idea of her being *equipped* to use the expression, and the analysis of *this* idea is also problematic.

So I shall for the present abandon the attempt to provide a definition, and content myself with a few informal remarks. There seem to me to be three main cases in which one may legitimately speak of an established procedure in respect of utterance-type X.

(1) That in which X is current for some group G; that is to say, to utter X in such-and-such circumstances is part of the practice of many members of G. In that case my Aunt Matilda (a member of G) may be said to have a procedure for X even though she herself would rather be seen dead than utter X; for she knows that some other members of G *do* have a readiness to utter X in such-and-such circumstances.

(2) That in which X is current only for U; it is only *U*'s practice to utter X in such-and-such circumstances. In this case U *will* have a readiness to utter X in such-and-such circumstances.

(3) That in which X is not current at all, but the utterance of X in such-and-such circumstances is part of some system of communication which U has devised, but which has never been put into operation (like the new Highway Code which I invent

one day while lying in my bath). In that case U has a procedure for X in the attenuated sense that he has envisaged a possible system of practices which *would* involve a readiness to utter X in such-and-such circumstances.

Stage IV   (Step (1): applied timeless meaning for unstructured utterance-types)

We are now in a position to define a notion of applied timeless meaning which will apply to H-W.

D.4. 'When U uttered X (type), X meant "$*$p" ' $=$ df. '($\exists$A) ($\exists$q) (U intended A to recognize (? and to recognize that U intended A to recognize) what U meant [occasion-meaning] by his uttering X, on the basis of A's knowledge (assumption) that, for U, X means (has as one of its meanings) "$*$p" [as defined by D.2.])'.

Or more fully:

Let '$*$' and '$*$'' both be dummy mood-indicators.

D.4'. 'When U uttered X, X meant "$*\psi$p" ' $=$ df. '($\exists$A) (U meant by uttering X that $*$'q; and U intended A to recognize (? and to recognize that he was intended to recognize) that by uttering X U meant that $*$'q *via* A's knowledge (assumption) that in U's repertoire is the procedure of uttering X if, for some A', U wants A' to $\psi^\dagger$ that p)'. ['p' may, or may not, represent that propositional content to which indefinite reference is made in the existential quantification of 'q'.]

D.4., and of course D.4'., allow both for the case in which U meant by H-W *that* he knew the route (coincidence of meaning '...' and meaning *that* ...), and also for the case in which, for example, U (a criminal) has lured a victim into his car and signals (non-literally, so to speak) to his accomplice that he knows how to handle the victim. In both cases it is expected by U that the audience's understanding of the utterance of H-W will be based on its knowledge that U has a certain procedure (to utter H-W if U wants an audience to think that U thinks U knows the route).

Stages III and IV   (Step (2): timeless and applied timeless meaning for structured utterance-types, complete and non-complete)

To deal with structure utterance-types and their elements, I think I need the following apparatus.

(1) Let '$\Sigma_1 (\Sigma_2)$' (read 'Σ_1-with-Σ_2') denote a sentence of which Σ_2 is a sub-sentence. Allow that a sentence is a sub-sentence of itself, and so that Σ_2 may $= \Sigma_1$.

(2) Let $v[\Sigma_1 (\Sigma_2)]$ (read 'v-of-Σ_1-with-Σ_2') be a particular utterance (token) of $\Sigma_1 (\Sigma_2)$ uttered by U. $v[\Sigma_1 (\Sigma_2)]$ is to be a *complete* utterance; that is, it is not to be part of $v[\Sigma_3 (\Sigma_1 (\Sigma_2))]$ (not e.g. to be the utterance of a disjunct).

(3) It is characteristic of sentences (a characteristic shared with phrases) that their standard meaning is consequential upon the meaning of the elements (words, lexical items) which enter into them. So I need the notion of a 'resultant procedure': as a first approximation, one might say that a procedure for an utterance-type X will be a resultant procedure if it is determined by (its existence is inferable from) a know-

ledge of procedures (a) for particular utterance-types which are elements in X, and (b) for any sequence of utterance-types which exemplifies a particular ordering of syntactical categories (a particular syntactical form).

Now let us deal with the notion of timeless meaning in U's idiolect.

D.5. 'For U, Σ means "$*\psi$p"' =df. 'U has a resultant procedure for Σ, viz. to utter Σ if, for some A, U wants A to ψ^+ that p.' [D.5. parallels D.2.]

An explication of timeless meaning in any language can, perhaps, be provided by adapting D.3.; I shall not attempt this task now.

For applied timeless meaning I offer

D.6. 'Σ_2 in v[Σ_1 (Σ_2)] meant "$*\psi$p"' =df. '(ijA) (ijq) (U meant by v[Σ_1 (Σ_2)] that $*$'q, and U intended A to recognize that U meant by v[Σ_1 (Σ_2)] that $*$'q at least partly on the basis of A's thought that U has a resultant procedure for Σ_2, viz. (for suitable A') to utter Σ_2 if U wants A' to ψ^+ that p).' [D.6. parallels D.4'.]

So far (maybe) so good. But the notion of 'resultant procedure' has been left pretty unilluminated; and if we are to shed any light on the notion of word-meaning, and its connection with 'meaning that', we ought to look at the nature of the more fundamental procedures from which a resultant procedure descends. It would be nice to give a general schema, to show the role of word-meanings (covering every type of word) in determining (in combination) sentence meanings (covering sentences of any syntactical structure). But this looks like a Herculean task (in our present state of knowledge). The best we can hope for is a sketch, for a very restricted (but central) range of word-types and syntactical forms, of a fragment of what might be the kind of theory we need. Let us take as our range all or part of the range of affirmative categorical (not necessarily indicative) sentences involving a noun (or definite description) and an adjective (or adjectival phrase).

The apparatus needed (for one such attempt) would be:

(1) Suppose σ to be an indicative sentence. Then we need to be able to apply the ideas of an indicative version of σ (σ itself), an imperative version of σ, an optative version of σ etc. (mood variations). It would be the business of some linguistic theory to equip us to apply such characterizations (so as philosophers of language we can assume this as given).

(2) We need to be able to apply some such notion as a predication of β (adjectival) on α (nominal). 'Smith is tactful', 'Smith, be tactful', 'Let Smith be tactful', 'Oh that Smith may be tactful' would be required to count, all of them, as predications of 'tactful' on 'Smith'. It would again be the business of some linguistic theory to set up such a sentential characterization.

(3) Suppose we, for a moment, take for granted two species of correlation, R-correlation (referential) and D-correlation (denotational). We want to be able to speak of some particular object as an R-correlate of α (nominal), and of each member of some class as being a D-correlate of β (adjectival).

Now suppose that U has the following procedures:

P.1. To utter the indicative version of σ if (for some A) U wants/intends A to think that U thinks ... (the blank being filled by the infinitive version of σ, e.g. 'Smith to be tactful'.) (Also, for example P.1': obtained from P.1 by substituting 'imperative'/ 'indicative' and 'intend'/'think that U thinks'.) [Such procedures set up correlations between moods and specifications of 'ψ^+'.]

P.2. To utter ψ^+-correlated [cf. P.1. and P.1'., etc.] predication of β on α if (for some A) U wants A to ψ^+ a particular R-correlate of α to be one of a particular set of D-correlates of β.

Further suppose that, for U, the following correlations hold:

C1. Jones' dog is an R-correlate of 'Fido'.

C2. Any hairy-coated thing is a D-correlate of 'shaggy'.

Given that U has the initial procedures P.1. and P.2. we can infer that U has the resultant procedure (determined by P.1. and P.2.): RP1. To utter the indicative version of a predication of β on α if U wants A to think U to think a particular R-correlate of α to be one of a particular set of D-correlates of β.

Given RP1 and C1 we can infer that U has

RP2. To utter the indicative version of a predication of β on 'Fido' if U wants A to think U to think Jones' dog to be one of a particular set of D-correlates of β.

Given RP2 and C2, we can infer that U has

RP3. To utter the indicative version of a predication of 'shaggy' on 'Fido' if U wants A to think U to think Jones' dog is one of the set of hairy-coated things (i.e. is hairy-coated).

And given the information from the linguist that 'Fido is shaggy' is the indicative version of a predication of 'shaggy' on 'Fido' (assumed), we can infer U to have

RP4. To utter 'Fido is shaggy' if U wants A to think U to think that Jones' dog is hairy-coated. And RP4. is an interpretant of 'For U, "Fido is shaggy" means "Jones' dog is hairy-coated".'

I have not yet provided an explication for statements of timeless meaning relating to non-complete utterance-types. I am not in a position to provide a definiens for 'X [non-complete] means "..."'; indeed I am not certain that a general form of definition *can* be provided for this schema; it may remain impossible to provide a definiens until the syntactical category of X has been given. I can, however, provide a definiens which may be adequate for *adjectival* X (e.g. 'shaggy').

D.7. 'For U, (adjectival) means "..."' =df. 'U has this procedure: to utter a ψ^+-correlated predication of X on α if (for some A) U wants A to ψ^+ a particular R-correlate of α to be...' [where the two lacunae represented by dots are identically completed].

Any specific procedure of the form mentioned in the definiens of D.7. can be shown to be a *resultant* procedure; for example, if U had P.2. and also C2., it will be inferable that he has the procedure of uttering a ψ^+-correlated predication of 'shaggy' on α if (for some A) U wants A to ψ^+ a particular R-correlate of α to be one of the set of hairy-coated things, i.e. that for U 'shaggy' means 'hairy-coated'.

I can now offer a definition of the notion of a *complete* utterance-type which has so far been taken for granted.

D.8. 'X is complete' =df. 'A fully expanded definiens for "X means '…'" contains no explicit reference to correlation, other than that involved in speaking of an R-correlate of some referring expression occurring within X'. [The expanded definiens for the complete utterance-type 'He is shaggy' may be expected to contain the phrase 'a particular R-correlate of "he".]

Correlation. We must now stop taking for granted the notion of correlation. What is it to mean to say that e.g. Jones' dog is the/a R-correlate of 'Fido'? One idea (building in as little as possible) would be to think of 'Fido' and Jones' dog as paired, in some system of pairing in which names and objects form ordered pairs. But in *one* sense of 'pair' any one name and any one object form a pair (an ordered pair, the first member of which is the name, the second the object). We want a sense of 'paired' in which 'Fido' is paired with Jones' dog but not with Smith's cat. 'Selected pair'? But what does 'selected' mean? Not 'selected' in the sense in which an apple and an orange may be selected from a dish: perhaps in the sense in which a dog may be selected (as something with which (to which) the selector intends to do something). But, in the case of the word-thing pair, do what? And what is the process of selecting?

I suggest we consider initially the special case in which linguistic and non-linguistic items are *explicitly* correlated. Let us take this to consist in performing some act as a result of which a linguistic item or a non-linguistic item (or items) come to stand in a relation in which they did not previously stand, and in which neither stands to non-correlates in the other realm. Since the act of correlation *may* be a verbal act, how can this set up a relation between items?

Suppose U produces a particular utterance (token) V, which belongs to the utterance-type 'shaggy: hairy-coated things'. To be able to say that U had by V correlated 'shaggy' with each member of the set of hairy-coated things, we should need to be able to say that there is some relation R such that:

(a) By uttering V, U effected that 'shaggy' stood in R to each hairy-coated thing, and only to hairy-coated things.

(b) U uttered V *in order that*, by uttering V he should effect this.

It is clear that condition (b), on which some will look askance because it introduces a reference to U's *intention* in performing his act of correlation, is required, and that condition (a) alone would be inadequate. Certainly by uttering V, regardless of his intentions, U has set up a situation in which a relation R holds exclusively between 'shaggy' and each hairy-coated thing Z, namely the relation which consists in being an expression uttered by U on a particular occasion O in conversational juxtaposition with the name of a class to which Z belongs. But, by the same act, U has also set up a situation in which another relation R′ holds exclusively between 'shaggy' and each *non*-hairy-coated thing Z′, namely the relation which consists in being an expression uttered by U on occasion O in conversational justaposition with the name of the *complement* of a class to which Z′ belongs. We do not, however, for our purposes, wish to think of U as having correlated 'shaggy' with each non-hairy-coated thing. The only way to ensure that R′ is eliminated is to add condition (b), which confines attention to a relationship which U *intends* to set up. It looks as if intensionality is embedded in the very foundations of the theory of language.

Let us, then, express more formally the proposed account of correlation. Suppose that V = utterance-token of type ' "Shaggy": hairy-coated things' (written). Then, by uttering V, U has correlated 'Shaggy' with (and only with) each hairy-coated thing ≡ (∃R) {(U effected by V that (Vx) (R 'Shaggy' x ≡ xy (y is a hairy-coated thing))) & (U uttered V in order that U effect by V that (Vx) ...)}.

If so understood, U will have correlated 'shaggy' with hairy-coated things only if there is an identifiable R′ for which the condition specified in the definiens holds. What is such an R′? I suggest R′xy ≡ x is a (word) type such that V is a sequence consisting of a token of x followed by a colon followed by an expression ['hairy-coated things'] the R-correlate of which is a set of which y is a member. R′xy holds between 'shaggy' and each hairy-coated thing given U's utterance of V. Any utterance V′ of the form exemplified by V could be uttered to set up R″xy (involving V′ instead of V) between any expression and each member of any set of non-linguistic items.

There are other ways of achieving the same effect. The purpose of making the utterance can be specified in the utterance: V = utterance of 'To effect that, for some R, "shaggy" has R only to each hairy-coated thing, "shaggy": hairy-coated things'. (The expression of the specified R will now have 'V is a sequence *containing*' vice 'V is a sequence *consisting of* ...'.) Or U can use the performative form: 'I correlate "shaggy" with each hairy-coated thing'. Utterance of this form will at the same time set up the required relation and label itself as being uttered with the purpose of setting up such a relation.

But by whichever form an act of explicit correlation is effected, to say of it that it is (or is intended to be) an act of correlation will always be to make an indefinite reference to a relation(ship) which the act is intended to set up, and the specification of the relation involved will in turn always involve a further use of the notion of correlation (e.g. as above in speaking of a set which is the correlate (R-correlate) of a particular expression (e.g. 'Hairy-coated things')). This seems to involve a regress which might well be objectionable; though 'correlation' is not used in definition of correlation, it will be used in specification of an indefinite reference occurring in the definition of correlation. It might be considered desirable (even necessary) to find a way of stopping this regress at some stage. (Is this a characteristically *empiricist* demand?) If we don't stop it, can correlation even get started (if prior correlation is presupposed?). Let us try 'ostensive correlation'.

(Acts 1, 2, 3, etc.) U ostends objects $\left\{\begin{matrix} a_1, \\ a_2, \\ a_3, \end{matrix}\right\}$ simultaneously with each ostension

uttering 'shaggy' (intending to ostend only objects which are hairy-coated). For the combination of these acts to constitute a case of correlating 'shaggy' with each hairy-coated thing, it must be the case that:

$\quad$ ($\exists$R) (U effected, and intended to effect, by acts 1, 2, 3, etc. that (Vy) ('Shaggy' has R to y if and only if y is hairy-coated)).

How is the appropriate relation to be specified? As follows:

$\quad$ R'xy (for some F) [viz. being hairy-coated] (U ostended and intended to ostend only objects which are F and, in acts 1, 2, 3, etc. accompanied each ostension by uttering a token of x; and y is F).

Given the ostensions, R'xy holds between 'shaggy' and each hairy-coated thing, and the specification of R'xy at least *seems* not to involve further reference to correlation.

So far, we have been acting on the assumption that the correlations, which in association with initial procedures yield further procedures, are explicit correlations; that is to say, that they are correlations set up by some identifiable and dateable act of correlating. But this assumption is clearly artificial. Many correlations, referential as well as denotative, seem to grow rather than to be created. The situation seems to be as follows:

(1) We need to be able to invoke such a resultant procedure as the following, which we will call RP12, namely, to predicate β on 'Fido', when U wants A to $\psi^\dagger$ that Jones' dog is a D-correlate of β; and we want to be able to say that at least sometimes such a resultant procedure may result from among other things a *non-explicit* R-correlation of 'Fido' and Jones' dog.

(2) It is tempting to suggest that a non-explicit R-correlation of 'Fido' and Jones' dog *consists* in the fact that U *would*, explicitly, correlate 'Fido' and Jones' dog.

(3) But to say that U would explicitly correlate 'Fido' and Jones' dog must be understood as an elliptical way of saying something of the form 'U would explicitly correlate "Fido" and Jones' dog, *if p*'. How is 'p' to be specified?

(4) Perhaps 'If U were asked to give an explicit correlation for "Fido" '. But if U were actually faced with a request, he might quite well take it that he is being asked to make a stipulation in making which he would have an entirely free hand. If he is not being asked for a stipulation, then it must be imparted to him that his explicit correlation is to satisfy some non-arbitrary condition. But what condition can this be? Again it is tempting to suggest that he is to make his explicit correlation such as to match or fit existing procedures.

(5) In application to RP12, this would seem to amount to imposing on U the demand that he should make his explicit correlation such as to yield RP12.

(6) In that case, RP12 results from a non-explicit correlation which consists in the

fact that U *would* explicitly correlate 'Fido' and Jones' dog if he wanted to make an explicit correlation which would generate relevant existing procedures, viz. RP12 itself. There is an apparent circularity here. Is this tolerable?

(7) It may be tolerable in as much as it may be a special case of a general phenomenon which arises in connection with the explanation of linguistic practice. We can, if we are lucky, identify 'linguistic rules', so called, which are such that our linguistic practice is *as if* we accepted these rules and consciously followed them. But we want to say that this is not just an interesting fact about our linguistic practice, but an explanation of it; and this leads us on to suppose that 'in some sense', 'implicity', we *do* accept these rules. Now the proper interpretation of the idea that we *do* accept these rules becomes something of a mystery, if the 'acceptance' of the rules is to be distinguished from the existence of the related practices; but it seems like a mystery which, for the time being at least, we have to swallow, while recognizing that it involves us in an as yet unsolved problem.

CONCLUDING NOTE

It will hardly have escaped notice that my account of the cluster of notions connected with the term 'meaning' has been studded with expressions for such intensional concepts as those of intending and of believing; and my partial excursions into symbolic notation have been made partly with the idea of revealing my commitment to the legitimacy of quantifying over such items as propositions. I shall make two highly general remarks about this aspect of my procedure.

(1) I am not sympathetic towards any methodological policy which would restrict one from the start in an attempt to formulate a theory of meaning in extensional terms. It seems to me that one should at least *start* by giving oneself a free hand to make use of any intensional notions or devices which seem to be required in order to solve one's conceptual problems, at least at a certain level, in ways which (metaphysical bias apart) reason and intuition commend. If one denies oneself this freedom, one runs a very serious risk of underestimating the richness and complexity of the conceptual field which one is investigating.

(2) I said at one point that intensionality seems to be embedded in the very foundations of the theory of language. Even if this appearance corresponds with reality, one is not, I suspect, precluded from being, in at least one important sense, an extensionalist. The psychological concepts which, in my view, are needed for the formulation of an adequate theory of language may not be among the most primitive or fundamental psychological concepts (like those which apply not only to human beings but to quite lowly animals as well); and it may be possible to derive (in *some* relevant sense of 'derive') the intensional concepts which I have been using from more primitive extensional concepts. Any extensionalist has to deal with the problem

of allowing for a transition from an extensional to a non-extensional language; and it is by no means obvious to me that intensionality can be explained only *via* the idea of concealed references to language, and so presupposes the concepts in terms of which the use of language will have to be understood.

V

TOPICS IN THE THEORY OF GENERATIVE GRAMMAR

NOAM CHOMSKY

(a) ASSUMPTIONS AND GOALS

My original intention was to use these lectures to present some recent work on general linguistic theory and on the structure of English, within the general framework of transformational generative grammar. However, a sequence of recent publications has indicated that many points that I had hoped to take for granted are widely regarded as controversial, and has also indicated misunderstanding, on a rather substantial scale, of the general framework I had expected to presuppose—in particular, a misunderstanding as to which elements of this framework express substantive assumptions about the nature of language and are, therefore, matters of legitimate controversy and rational discussion, and which, on the other hand, relate only to questions of goals and interests and are therefore no more subject to debate than the question: is chemistry right or wrong? In the light of this, it seems advisable to change my original plan and to spend much more time on background assumptions and general questions of various sorts than I had at first intended. I still hope to be able to incorporate an exposition (much abbreviated) of some recent work, but I will lead up to it more slowly, in the following steps:

(1) discussion of general background assumptions and goals that underlie and motivate much of the work in generative grammar of the past decade;

(2) discussion of various objections to this general point of view that seem to me to be based on error, misunderstanding, or equivocation of one sort or another;

(3) presentation of a theory of generative grammar of a sort exemplified, for example, in N. Chomsky, *Syntactic Structures* (The Hague, 1957), R. B. Lees, *The Grammar of English Nominalizations* (Bloomington, 1960), M. Halle, 'Phonology in a Generative Grammar', *Word*, 18, pp. 54–72 (1962), and J. Katz and J. Fodor, 'The Structure of a Semantic Theory', *Lg.* 39, pp. 170–210 (1963);

(4) discussion of various real inadequacies that have been exposed in this position in work of the past half-dozen years; and

(5) sketch of a refined and improved version of this theory, designed to overcome these difficulties.

From *Topics in the Theory of Generative Grammar* (in *Janua Linguarum*), (Mouton & Co., The Hague, 1966), pp. 7–24 and 51–75. Reprinted by permission of the author, the editor, and the publishers.

I will try to cover these points in the first three sections, concentrating largely on syntax. Section I will deal with the first point, section II with the second, and section III with the third, fourth and fifth.*

In the final section I will discuss an approach to the study of sound structure that has been gradually evolving since Chomsky, Halle, and F. Lukoff, 'On Accent and Juncture in English', *For Roman Jakobson,* eds. M. Halle, H. Lunt, and H. MacLean, pp. 65–80 (The Hague, 1956), and has been presented in various stages of development in publications of Halle's and mine (listed in the bibliography below) since then, and will, hopefully, soon emerge to full light of day in a book that is now in active preparation. In the course of this presentation, I will also discuss a few criticisms of this approach. The discussion of criticisms will be very brief, however, since Halle and I have discussed most of them, in so far as they are known to us, in considerable detail elsewhere.[1]

In general, this essay contains no new or original material. it is intended only as an informal guide to other books and papers,[2] in which questions touched on here are dealt with more thoroughly, and as an attempt to clarify issues that have been raised in critical discussion.

In the course of this paper I will also make a few remarks about historical back-. grounds for the position that will be outlined.[3] Quite a few commentators have assumed that recent work in generative grammar is somehow an outgrowth of an interest in the use of computers for one or another purpose, or that it has some other engineering motivation, or that it perhaps constitutes some obscure branch of mathematics. This view is incomprehensible to me, and it is, in any event, entirely false. Much more perceptive are those critics who have described this work as in large measure a return to the concerns and often even the specific doctrines of traditional linguistic theory. This is true—apparently to an extent that many critics do not realize.[4] I differ from them only in regarding this observation not as a criticism, but

---

* This volume includes section I and section III of the original marked (a) and (b) respectively [ed.].

[1] In particular, see Chomsky, *Current Issues in Linguistic Theory,* 31, pp. 105–7 (The Hague, 1964), which deals with criticisms in C. A. Ferguson's review of Halle, *The Sound Pattern of Russian* (The Hague, 1959); and in Chomsky and Halle, 'Some Controversial Questions in Phonological Theory', *Journal of Linguistics,* 1, pp. 97–138 (1965), which deals with objections raised by F. W. Householder Jr., 'On Some Recent Claims in Phonological Theory', *Journal of Linguistics,* 1, pp. 13–34 (1965).

[2] e.g. Katz and P. Postal, *An Integrated Theory of Linguistic Description* (Cambridge, Mass., 1964); Chomsky, *Current Issues in Linguistic Theory,* and *Aspects of the Theory of Syntax* (Cambridge, Mass., 1965).

[3] This matter is discussed in more detail in Chomsky, *Current Issues in Linguistic Theory,* § 1, in *Aspects of the Theory of Syntax,* Ch. 1, § 8, and in *Cartesian Linguistics* (New York, 1966).

[4] To cite just one example, consider A. Reichling, 'Principles and Methods of Syntax: Cryptanalytical Formalism', *Lingua* 10, pp. 1–7 (1961), who asserts that obviously I could not 'be said to sympathize with such a "mentalistic monster" as the "innere Sprachform"'. But in fact the work that he is discussing is quite explicitly and selfconsciously mentalistic (in the traditional, not the Bloomfieldian, sense of this word—that is, it is an attempt to construct a theory of mental processes), and it can, furthermore, be quite accurately described as an attempt to develop further the Humboldtian notion of 'form of language' and its implications for cognitive psychology, as will surely be evident to anyone familiar both with Humboldt and with recent work in generative grammar (for explicit discussion, see the references cited above).

rather as a definite merit of this work. That is, it seems to me that it is the modern study of language prior to the explicit study of generative grammar that is seriously defective in its failure to deal with traditional questions and, furthermore, to recognize the essential correctness of many of the traditional answers and the extent to which they provide a fruitful basis for current research.

A distinction must be made between what the speaker of a language knows implicitly (what we may call his *competence*) and what he does (his *performance*). A grammar, in the traditional view, is an account of competence. It describes and attempts to account for the ability of a speaker to understand an arbitrary sentence of his language and to produce an appropriate sentence on a given occasion. If it is a pedagogic grammar, it attempts to provide the student with this ability; if a linguistic grammar, it aims to discover and exhibit the mechanisms that make this achievement possible. The competence of the speaker-hearer can, ideally, be expressed as a system of rules that relate signals to semantic interpretations of these signals. The problem for the grammarian is to discover this system of rules; the problem for linguistic theory is to discover general properties of any system of rules that may serve as the basis for a human language, that is, to elaborate in detail what we may call, in traditional terms, the general *form of language* that underlies each particular realization, each particular natural language.

Performance provides evidence for the investigation of competence. At the same time, a primary interest in competence entails no disregard for the facts of performance and the problem of explaining these facts. On the contrary, it is difficult to see how performance can be seriously studied except on the basis of an explicit theory of the competence that underlies it, and, in fact, contributions to the understanding of performance have largely been by-products of the study of grammars that represent competence.[5]

Notice, incidentally, that a person is not generally aware of the rules that govern sentence-interpretation in the language that he knows; nor, in fact, is there any reason to suppose that the rules can be brought to consciousness. Furthermore, there is no reason to expect him to be fully aware even of the empirical consequences of these internalized rules—that is, of the way in which signals are assigned semantic interpretations by the rules of the language that he knows (and, by definition, knows perfectly). On the difficulties of becoming aware of one's own linguistic intuitions, see the discussion in Chomsky, *Aspects of the Theory of Syntax*, Ch. 1, § 4. It is

---

I will not consider Reichling's criticisms of generative grammar here. The cited remark is just one illustration of his complete lack of comprehension of the goals, concerns, and specific content of the work that he was discussing, and his discussion is based on such gross misrepresentation of this work that comment is hardly called for.

[5] For discussion, see G. A. Miller and Chomsky, 'Finitary Models of Language Users', *Handbook of Mathematical Psychology*, vol. II, eds. R. D. Luce, R. Bush, and E. Galanter (New York, 1963); Chomsky, *Aspects of the Theory of Syntax*, Ch. 1, § 2.

important to realize that there is no paradox in this; in fact, it is precisely what should be expected.

Current work in generative grammar has adopted this traditional framework of interests and concerns. It attempts to go beyond traditional grammar in a fundamental way, however. As has repeatedly been emphasized, traditional grammars make an essential appeal to the intelligence of the reader. They do not actually formulate the rules of the grammar, but rather give examples and hints that enable the intelligent reader to determine the grammar, in some way that is not at all understood. They do not provide an analysis of the 'faculté de langage' that makes this achievement possible. To carry the study of language beyond its traditional bounds, it is necessary to recognize this limitation and to develop means to transcend it. This is the fundamental problem to which all work in generative grammar has been addressed.

The most striking aspect of linguistic competence is what we may call the 'creativity of language', that is, the speaker's ability to produce new sentences, sentences that are immediately understood by other speakers although they bear no physical resemblance to sentences which are 'familiar'. The fundamental importance of this creative aspect of normal language use has been recognized since the seventeenth century at least, and it was at the core of Humboldtian general linguistics. Modern linguistics, however, is seriously at fault in its failure to come to grips with this central problem. In fact, even to speak of the hearer's 'familiarity with sentences' is an abusrdity. Normal use of language involves the production and interpretation of sentences that are similar to sentences that have been heard before only in that they are generated by the rules of the same grammar, and thus the only sentences that can in any serious sense be called 'familiar' are clichés or fixed formulas of one sort or another. The extent to which this is true has been seriously underestimated even by those linguists (e.g. O. Jespersen) who have given some attention to the problem of creativity. This is evident from the common description of language use as a matter of 'grammatical habit' (e.g. O. Jespersen, *Philosophy of Grammar* (London, 1924)). It is important to recognize that there is no sense of 'habit' known to psychology in which this characterization of language use is true (just as there is no notion of 'generalization' known to psychology or philosophy that entitles us to characterize the new sentences of ordinary linguistic usage as generalizations of previous performance). The familiarity of the reference to normal language use as a matter of 'habit' or as based on 'generalization' in some fundamental way must not blind one to the realization that these characterizations are simply untrue if terms are used in any technical or well-defined sense, and that they can be accepted only as metaphors— highly misleading metaphors, since they tend to lull the linguist into the entirely erroneous belief that the problem of accounting for the creative aspect of normal language use is not after all a very serious one.

Returning now to the central topic, a *generative grammar* (that is, an explicit grammar that makes no appeal to the reader's 'faculté de langage' but rather attempts to incorporate the mechanisms of this faculty) is a system of rules that relate signals to semantic interpretations of these signals. It is *descriptively adequate* to the extent that this pairing corresponds to the competence of the idealized speaker-hearer. The idealization is (in particular) that in the study of grammar we abstract away from the many other factors (e.g. memory limitations, distractions, changes of intention in the course of speaking, etc.) that interact with underlying competence to produce actual performance.

If a generative grammar is to pair signals with semantic interpretations, then the theory of generative grammar must provide a general, language-independent means for representing the signals and semantic interpretations that are interrelated by the grammars of particular languages. This fact has been recognized since the origins of linguistic theory, and traditional linguistics made various attempts to develop theories of universal phonetics and universal semantics that might meet this requirement. Without going into any detail, I think it would be widely agreed that the general problem of universal phonetics is fairly well understood (and has been, in fact, for several centuries), whereas the problems of universal semantics still remain veiled in their traditional obscurity. We have fairly reasonable techniques of phonetic representation that seem to approach adequacy for all known languages, though, of course, there is much to learn in this domain. In contrast, the immediate prospects for universal semantics seem much more dim, though surely this is no reason for the study to be neglected (quite the opposte conclusion should, obviously, be drawn). In fact, recent work of Katz, Fodor, and Postal, to which I return in the third section, seems to me to suggest new and interesting ways to reopen these traditional questions.

The fact that universal semantics is in a highly unsatisfactory state does not imply that we must abandon the programme of constructing grammars that pair signals and semantic interpretations. For although there is little that one can say about the language-independent system of semantic representation, a great deal is known about conditions that semantic representations must meet, in particular cases. Let us then introduce the neutral technical notion of 'syntactic description', and take a syntactic description of a sentence to be an (abstract) object of some sort, associated with the sentence, that uniquely determines its semantic interpretation (the latter notion being left unspecified pending further insights into semantic theory)[6] as well as its phonetic form. A particular linguistic theory must specify the set of possible syntactic descriptions for sentences of a natural language. The extent to which these syntactic descriptions meet the conditions that we know must apply to semantic interpretations provides one measure of the success and sophistication of the grammatical theory in question. As the theory of generative grammar has progressed, the notion of syntactic

---

[6] Working in this framework then, we would regard a semantically ambiguous minimal element as constituting two distinct lexical entries; hence two syntactic descriptions might differ only in that they contain different members of a pair of homonymous morphemes.

description has been clarified and extended. I will discuss below some recent ideas on just what should constitute the syntactic description of a sentence, if the theory of generative grammar is to provide descriptively adequate grammars.

Notice that a syntactic description (henceforth, SD) may convey information about a sentence beyond its phonetic form and semantic interpretation. Thus we should expect a descriptively adequate grammar of English to express the fact that the expressions (1)–(3) are ranked in the order given in terms of 'degree of deviation' from English, quite apart from the question of how interpretations can be imposed on them [in the case of (2) and (3)]:

(1)   the dog looks terrifying
(2)   the dog looks barking
(3)   the dog looks lamb

A generative grammar, then, must at least determine a pairing of signals with SD's; and a theory of generative grammar must provide a general characterization of the class of possible signals (a theory of phonetic representation) and the class of possible SD's. A grammar is descriptively adequate to the extent that it is factually correct in a variety of respects, in particular, to the extent that it pairs signals with SD's that do in fact meet empirically given conditions on the semantic interpretations that they support. For example, if a signal has two intrinsic semantic interpretations in a particular language [e.g. (4) or (5), in English], a grammar of this language will approach descriptive adequacy if it assigns two SD's to the sentence, and, beyond this, it will approach descriptive adequacy to the extent that these SD's succeed in expressing the basis for the ambiguity.

(4)   they don't know how good meat tastes
(5)   what disturbed John was being disregarded by everyone

In the case of (4), for example, a descriptively adequate grammar must not only assign two SD's to the sentence but must also do so in such a way that in one of these the grammatical relations of *good*, *meat*, and *taste* are as in 'meat tastes good', while in the other they are as in 'meat which is good tastes Adjective' (where the notion 'grammatical relation' is to be defined in a general way within the linguistic theory in question), this being the basis for the alternative semantic interpretations that may be assigned to this sentence. Similarly, in the case of (5), it must assign to the pair *disregard-John* the same grammatical relation as in 'everyone disregards John', in one SD; whereas in the other it must assign this very same relation to the pair *disregard-what* (*disturbed John*), and must assign no semantically functional grammatical relation at all to *disregard-John*. On the other hand, in the case of (6) and (7) only one SD should be assigned by a descriptively adequately grammar. This SD should, in the case of (6), indicate that *John* is related to *incompetent* as it is in 'John is incompetent', and that *John* is related to *regard* (*as incompetent*) as it is in 'everyone regards John as incompetent'. In the case of (7), the SD must indicate that *our* is related to *regard* (*as incompetent*) as *us* is related to *regard* (*as incompetent*) in 'everyone regards us an incompetent'.

(6)   what disturbed John was being regarded
                        as incompetent by everyone.
(7)   what disturbed John was our being regarded
                        as incompetent by everyone.

Similarly, in the case of (8), the grammar must assign four distinct SD's, each of which specifies the system of grammatical relations that underlies one of the distinct semantic interpretations of this sentence:

(8)   the police were ordered to stop drinking after midnight.

Examples such as these should suffice to illustrate what is involved in the problem of constructing descriptively adequate generative grammars and developing a theory of grammar that analyses and studies in full generality the concepts that appear in these particular grammars. It is quite evident from innumerable examples of this sort that the conditions on semantic interpretations are sufficiently clear and rich so that the problem of defining the notion 'syntactic description' and developing descriptively adequate grammars (relative to this notion of SD) can be made quite concrete, despite the fact that the notion 'semantic interpretation' itself still resists any deep analysis. We return to some recent ideas on semantic interpretation of SD's in section III.

A grammar, once again, must pair signals and SD's. The SD assigned to a signal must determine the semantic interpretation of the signal, in some way which, in detail, remains unclear. Furthermore, each SD must uniquely determine the signal of which it is the SD (uniquely, that is, up to free variation). Hence the SD must (i) determine a semantic interpretation and (ii) determine a phonetic representation. Let us define the 'deep structure of a sentence' as that aspect of the SD that determines its semantic interpretation, and the 'surface structure of a sentence' as that aspect of the SD that determines its phonetic form. A grammar, then, must consist of three components: a *syntactic component*, which generates SD's each of which consists of a surface structure and a deep structure; a *semantic component*, which assigns a semantic interpretation to a deep structure; a *phonological component*, which assigns a phonetic interpretation to a surface structure. Thus the grammar as a whole will associate phonetic representations and semantic interpretations, as required, this association being mediated by the syntactic component that generates deep and surface structures as elements of SD's.

The notions 'deep structure' and 'surface structure' are intended as explications of the Humboldtian notions 'inner form of a sentence' and 'outer form of a sentence' (the general notion 'form' is probably more properly to be related to the notion 'generative grammar' itself—cf. Chomsky, *Current Issues in Linguistic Theory*, for discussion). The terminology is suggested by the usage familiar in contemporary analytic philosophy (cf., for example, Wittgenstein, *Philosophical Investigations*, p. 168 (Oxford, 1953)). C. F. Hockett has also used these terms (*A Course in Modern Linguistics*, Ch. 29 (New York, 1958)) in roughly the same sense.

There is good reason (see below, section IV) to suppose that the surface structure of a sentence is a labelled bracketing that segments it into its continuous constituents, categorizes these, segments the constituents into further categorized constituents, etc. Thus underlying (6), for example, is a surface structure that analyses it into its constituents (perhaps, 'what disturbed John', 'was', 'being regarded as incompetent by everyone'), assigning each of these to a certain category indicated by the labelling, then further segmenting each of these into its constituents (e.g. perhaps, 'what disturbed John' into 'what' and 'disturbed John'), each of these being assigned to a category indicated by the labelling, etc., until ultimate constituents are reached. Information of this sort is, in fact, necessary to determine the phonetic representation of this sentence. The labelled bracketing can be presented in a tree-diagram, or in other familiar notations.

It is clear, however, that the deep structure must be quite different from this surface structure. For one thing, the surface representation in no way expresses the grammatical relations that are, as we have just observed, crucial for semantic interpretation. Secondly, in the case of an ambiguous sentence such as, for example, (5), only a single surface structure may be assigned, but the deep structures must obviously differ. Such examples as these are sufficient to indicate that the deep structure underlying a sentence cannot be simply a labelled bracketing of it. Since there is good evidence that the surface structure should, in fact, simply be a labelled bracketing, we conclude that deep structures cannot be identified with surface structures. The inability of surface structure to indicate semantically significant grammatical relations (i.e. to serve as deep structure) is one fundamental fact that motivated the development of transformational generative grammar, in both its classical and modern varieties.

In summary, a full generative grammar must consist of a syntactic, semantic, and phonological component. The syntactic component generates SD's each of which contains a deep structure and a surface structure. The semantic component assigns a semantic interpretation to the deep structure and the phonological component assigns a phonetic interpretation to the surface structure. An ambiguous sentence has several SD's, differing in the deep structures that they contain (though the converse need not be true).

So far I have said little that is in any way controversial. This discussion has so far simply delimited a certain domain of interest and a certain class of problems, and has suggested a natural framework for dealing with these problems. The only substantive comments (i.e. factual assertions) that I have so far made within the framework are that the surface structure is a labelled bracketing and that deep structures must in general be distinct from surface structures. The first of these assertions is well supported (see below), and would probably be widely accepted. The second is surely much too obvious to require elaborate defence.

To go on from here to develop a substantive linguistic theory we must provide:

(9)   (i)   theories of phonetic and semantic representation
      (ii) a general account of the notion 'syntactic description'
      (iii) a specification of the class of potential generative grammars
      (iv) a general account of how these grammars function, that is, how they generate SD's and assign to them phonetic and semantic interpretations, thus pairing phonetically represented signals with semantic interpretations.

Before going on to discuss these substantive questions, let us reassure ourselves about the uncontroversial character of what has preceded. Is there, in fact, anything in this account to which exception can be taken? Surely there is no conceivable question about the necessity for distinguishing competence from performance in the way suggested above. Having made this distinction, one may or may not choose to be interested in the general question of accounting for linguistic competence. If one chooses to concern himself with this question, he must immediately face the fact of 'creativity' and must therefore focus attention on the problem of constructing generative grammars. It is difficult to see how a full generative grammar can be regarded, ultimately, as anything other than a system of rules that relate signals to semantic interpretations; and, having set this goal, one is immediately faced with the problem of developing a rich enough notion of 'syntactic description' to support phonetic interpretation, on the one side, and semantic interpretation, on the other. The distinction between deep and surface structure emerges from even the most superficial examination of real linguistic material. Hence the conclusions outlined so far seem inescapable if the the problem of studying linguistic competence is taken up. Notice that a substantive linguistic theory involves a specification of (9iv) as well as (9iii). For example, an essential part of the theory of phrase-structure grammar is a particular specification of how categories and relations are determined for generated strings (see Chomsky, 'Logical Structure of Linguistic Theory', Cambridge, 1955, Ch. VI), and such a specification has been presupposed whenever this theory has been investigated. A change in this specification is as much a revision of the theory as a change in the specification of the class (9iii) of potential grammars. Failure to understand this leads to immediate absurdities. Thus if one thinks of the theory of 'phrase-structure' with the technique of interpretation (9iv) left free, one can easily prove that a phrase-structure grammar of the language L assigns to sentences of L the structural descriptions assigned by some transformational grammar of L, etc. This point should be obvious without further discussion.

Suppose that one chooses not to study linguistic competence (and, concomitantly, linguistic performance within the framework of a theory of competence). One might, alternatively, choose to limit attention to performance, or to surface structures, or to sound patterns in isolation from syntactic structure, or to voiced fricatives, or to first halves of sentences. The only question that arises, if any of these proposals is adopted, is whether any interesting result is likely to be attainable under such arbitrary limitation of subject matter. In each of the cited cases it seems quite un-unlikely. It is, in general, unclear why anyone should insist on studying an isolated aspect of the general problem of grammatical description unless there is some reason to believe that this is not affected by the character of other aspects of grammar.[7]

I have been discussing so far only the question of descriptive adequacy of grammars and the problem of developing a linguistic theory that will provide the basis for the construction of descriptively adequate grammars. As has been repeatedly empha-sized, however (see, e.g., Chomsky, *Syntactic Structures*; 'Explanatory Models in Linguistics', *Logic, Methodology, and Philosophy of Science,* eds. E. Nagel, P. Suppes, and A. Tarski (Stanford, 1962), pp. 528–50; *Current Issues in Linguistic Theory*; and *Aspects of the Theory of Syntax*), the goals of linguistic theory can be set much higher than this; and, in fact, it is a prerequisite even for the study of des-criptive adequacy that they be set higher than this. It is essential also to raise the question of 'explanatory adequacy' of linguistic theory. The nature of this question can be appreciated readily in terms of the problem of constructing a hypothetical language-acquisition device AD that can provide as 'output' a descriptively adequate grammar G for the language L on the basis of certain primary linguistic data from L as an input; that is, a device represented schematically as (10):

(10)   primary linguistic data $\rightarrow \boxed{\text{AD}} \rightarrow$ G

[7] Perhaps this matter can be clarified by considering examples of the latter sort. Thus, for example, it is quite reasonable to study semantics in isolation from phonology or phonology in isolation from semantics, since, at the moment, there seems to be no non-trivial relation between the systems of phonological and semantic interpretation and no significant way in which semantic considerations can play a role in phonology or phonological considerations in semantics. Similarly, it seems quite reasonable to develop a theory of syntactic structure with no primitive notions of an essentially semantic nature, since, at the moment, there is no reason to assume that *a priori* semantic concepts play a role in determining the organization of the syntactic component of a grammar. On the other hand, it would be absurd to study semantics (and similarly, it seems to me, phonology) in isolation from syntax, since the syntactic interpretation of a sentence (similarly, its phonetic interpretation) depends in an essential way on its deep (respectively, surface) structure. And it would be absurd to develop general syntactic theory without assigning an absolutely crucial role to semantic considerations, since obviously the necessity to support semantic interpretation is one of the primary requirements that the structures generated by the syntactic component of a grammar must meet. For discussion of these points, see Chomsky, *Syntactic Structures* and *Current Issues in Linguistic Theory*; Lees, Review of Chomsky, *Syntactic Structures, Lg.,* pp. 375–408 (1957); Katz and Postal, *An Integrated Theory of Linguistic Description,* and many other references.

Far too little care has been taken in the discussion of these questions in modern linguistics. As a result, there has been much confusion about them, and many dogmatic claims have been voiced and repeatedly echoed with no attempt to justify or support them by serious argument. The issues are important; while no answers to any of these questions can be given with any certainty, the tentative position that the linguist accepts may have an important influence on the character of the work that he does.

We naturally want the device AD to be language-independent—that is, capable of learning any human language and only these. We want it, in other words, to provide an implicit definition of the notion 'human language'. Were we able to develop the specifications for a language-acquisition device of this sort, we could realistically claim to be able to provide an explanation for the linguistic intuition—the tacit competence—of the speaker of a language. This explanation would be based on the assumption that the specifications of the device AD provide the basis for language-acquisition, primary linguistic data from some language providing the empirical conditions under which the development of a generative grammar takes place. The difficulties of developing an empirically adequate language-independent specification of AD are too obvious to require extended discussion; the vital importance of raising this problem and pursuing it intensively at every stage of linguistic investigation also seems to me entirely beyond the possibility of debate (cf. the references cited above for elaboration of this point).

To pursue the study of explanatory adequacy, we may proceed in two parallel ways. First, we must attempt to provide as narrow a specification of the aspects of linguistic theory listed in (9) as is compatible with the known diversity of languages—we must, in other words, develop as rich a hypothesis concerning linguistic universals as can be supported by available evidence. This specification can then be attributed to the system AD as an intrinsic property. Second, we may attempt to develop a general evaluation procedure, as an intrinsic property of AD, which will enable it to select a particular member of the class of grammars that meet the specifications (9) (or, conceivably, to select a small set of alternatives, though this abstract possibility is hardly worth discussing for the present) on the basis of the presented primary linguistic data. This procedure will then enable the device to select one of the *a priori* possible hypotheses—one of the permitted grammars—that is compatible with the empirically given data from a given language. Having selected such a hypothesis, it has 'mastered' the language described by this grammar (and it thus knows a great deal beyond what it has explicitly 'learned'). Given a linguistic theory that specifies (9) and an evaluation procedure, we can explain some of the aspect of the speaker's competence whenever we can show with some plausibility that this aspect of his competence is determined by the most highly valued grammar of the permitted sort that is compatible with data of the kind to which he has actually been exposed.

Notice that an evaluation procedure (simplicity measure, as it is often called in technical discussion) is itself an empirical hypothesis concerning universal properties of language; it is, in other words, a hypothesis, true or false, about the prerequisites for language-acquisition. To support or refute this hypothesis, we must consider evidence as to the factual relation between primary linguistic data and descriptively adequate grammars. We must ask whether the proposed evaluation procedure in fact can mediate this empirically given relation. An evaluation procedure, therefore, has much the status of a physical constant; in particular, it is impossible to support or reject a specific proposal on the basis of *a priori* argument.

Once again, it is important to recognize that there is nothing controversial in what has just been said. One may or may not choose to deal with the problem of explanatory adequacy. One who chooses to overlook this problem may (and, in my opinion, surely will) find that he has eliminated from consideration one of the most important sources of evidence bearing on the problems that remain (in particular, the problem of descriptive adequacy).[8] His situation, then, may be quite analogous to that of the person who has decided to limit his attention to surface structures (to the exclusion of deep structures) or to first halves of sentences. He must show that the delimitation of interest leaves him with a viable subject. But, in any event, he surely has no basis for objecting to the attempt on the part of other linguists to study the general question of which he has (artificially, in my opinion) delimited one facet.

I hope that these remarks will be sufficient to show the complete pointlessness of much of the debate over the specific evaluation procedures (simplicity measures) that have been proposed as empirical hypotheses concerning the form of language in the course of work in generative grammar. To mention just one example, consider Householder's criticism (Householder, 'On Some Recent Claims in Phonological Theory', *Journal of Linguistics,* I (1965), pp. 13–34) of several proposals of Halle's regarding an appropriate evaluation procedure for phonology. Halle presented a certain theory of phonological processes, including, as an essential part, a certain empirical hypothesis regarding a simplicity measure. A crucial aspect of this theory was its complete reliance on distinctive features in the formulation of phonological rules to the exclusion of any 'segmental' notation (e.g. phonemic notation) except as an informal expository device. His evaluation measure involved minimization of features in the lexicon and the phonological rules. In support of this theory he showed that a variety of facts can be explained on these assumptions. He also discussed alternative theories that use segmental notation along with or instead of feature notation and gave several arguments to show that under these assumptions it is difficult to see how any empirically valid evaluation measure can be formulated

---

[8] The reason for this is quite simple. Choice of a descriptively adequate grammar for the language L is always much underdetermined (for the linguist, that is) by data from L. Other relevant data can be adduced from study of descriptively adequate grammars of other languages, but only if the linguist has an explanatory theory of the sort just sketched. Such a theory can receive empirical support from its success in providing descriptively adequate grammars for other languages. Furthermore, it prescribes, in advance, the form of the grammar of L and the evaluation procedure that leads to the selection of this grammar, given data. In this way, it permits data from other languages to play a role in justifying the grammar selected as an empirical hypothesis concerning the speakers of L. This approach is quite natural. Following it, the linguist comes to a conclusion about the speakers of L on the basis of an independently supported assumption about the nature of language in general—an assumption, that is, concerning the general 'faculté de language' that makes language-acquisition possible. The general explanatory theory of language and the specific theory of a particular language that results from application of the general theory to data each has psychological content, the first as a hypothesis about innate mental structure, the second as a hypothesis about the tacit knowledge that emerges with exposure to appropriate experience.

—in particular, he showed how various rather natural measures involving minimization fail on empirical grounds.

Householder makes no attempt to refute these arguments but simply objects to them because they fail to meet certain *a priori* conditions that he arbitrarily imposes on any notion of 'evaluation procedure', in particular, the requirement that such a procedure must favour grammars that use fewer symbols and that are easy for the linguist to read. Since the grammars that Halle proposes, with their consistent reliance on feature representation, require more symbols than grammars that use auxiliary symbols as abbreviations for feature sets, and since Halle's grammars are (Householder claims) not easy to read, he concludes that the theory on which they are based must be mistaken. But clearly *a priori* arguments of this sort have no bearing on an empirical hypothesis about the nature of language (i.e. about the structure of a general language-acquisition device of the sort described above). Consequently, Householder's critique has no relevance to any issue that Halle discusses. Unfortunately, much of the criticism of recent attempts to develop valid evaluation measures is based on similar presuppositions.

Notice, incidentally, that there is an interesting but poorly understood sense in which one can talk of the 'simplicity' or 'elegance' or 'naturalness' of a theory (of language, of the chemical bond, etc.), but this 'absolute' sense of simplicity has no clear relevance to the attempt to develop an evaluation measure (a simplicity measure) as a part of a theory of grammar. Such a theory is an empirical hypothesis, true or false, proposed to account for some domain of linguistic fact. The 'simplicity measure' that it contains is a constituent part of this empirical hypothesis. This distinction between 'simplicity' as an absolute notion of general epistemology and 'simplicity' as a part of a theory of grammar has been repeatedly emphasized; confusion regarding this point has, nevertheless, been quite widespread. Failure to make this distinction vitiates most of the criticism of evaluation procedures that has appeared in recent years.

(b) THE THEORY OF TRANSFORMATIONAL GENERATIVE GRAMMAR

HAVING now covered the first two parts of the outline given in the introductory section, I would like to turn, much more briefly, to parts three, four, and five. These are discussed in much more detail in Chomsky, *Aspects of the Theory of Syntax*, and in the references cited there.

The earliest versions of transformational generative grammar made the following general assumptions concerning syntactic structure. The syntactic component of a grammar consists of two sorts of rules: rewriting rules and transformational rules. The rewriting rules constitute a phrase-structure grammar (with, perhaps, a condition of linear ordering imposed). Each rule is, in other words, of the form A→X (with a possible restriction to the context Z—W), where A is a category symbol and X, Z, W are strings of category or terminal symbols. The strings generated by this system we may call *base strings* (an alternative term is *C-terminal strings*). In the course of generating a string, the system of rewriting rules (let us call this the *base component* of the syntax) assigns to it a phrase-marker which we can call a *base phrase-marker*, this being representable as a labelled bracketing or a tree diagram with categories labelling the nodes.

The transformational rules map phrase-markers into new, derived phase-markers. Each transformational rule is defined by a *structural analysis* stating a condition on the class of phrase-markers to which it applies and specifying an analysis of the terminal string of this phrase-marker into successive parts. The specification of the transformation is completed by associating with this structural analysis a certain *elementary transformation* which is a formal operation on strings, of a certain narrow class. For details, see the references cited above. By defining the 'product' of two phrase-markers as the new phrase-marker derived essentially by concatenation of the labelled bracketings,[9] we can apply what have been called *generalized* (or *double base, triple base* etc.) transformations to a phrase-marker representing a sequence of phrase-markers, mapping such a product into a new phrase-marker by the same apparatus as is required in the singulary case. The transformations meet certain ordering conditions (I return to these below), which must be stated in a separate part of the grammar. These conditions include a specification of certain transformation as *obligatory* or obligatory relative to certain sequences of transformations. To generate a sentence, we select a sequence of (one or more) base phrase-markers and apply singulary and generalized transformations to them, observing the ordering and obligatoriness requirements, until the result is a single phrase-marker dominated by S (the *initial category*, representing 'sentence'). If we select a single base phrase-marker and apply only obligatory transformations, we call the resulting sentence a *kernel sentence* (a kernel sentence is not to be confused with the base string that underlies it as well as possibly many other more complex sentences).

We can represent the system of transformations that apply in the process of derivation as a transformation-marker (T-marker). To illustrate, consider the sentence

(18)   I expected the man who quit work to be fired.

---

[9] Precise definitions of the notions mentioned here are provided in Chomsky, 'The Logical Structure of Linguistic Theory', unpublished manuscript, Microfilm M.I.T. Library (Cambridge, Mass., 1955), and descriptions of varying degrees of informality appear throughout the literature. In particular, a phrase-marker is representable as a set of strings, and the 'product' of two phrase-markers is then the complex product of the two sets (i.e. the set of all strings XY such that X is in the first set and Y in the second).

The transformational derivation of (18) might be represented by the T-Marker (19). In this representation, B_1, B_2 and B_3 are the three base phrase-markers that underlie the (kernel) sentences (20i)–(20iii):[10]

(19)

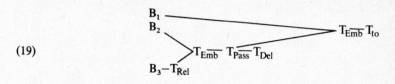

(20)

        (i) I expected it
       (ii) someone fired the man
     (iii) the man quit work

The interpretation of (19) is straightforward. It represents the fact that to form (18) we take the three base structures underlying (20i–iii), and proceed as follows. First, apply to B_3 the relative transformation T_{Rel} that converts it to 'who (the man) quit work' (rather, to the abstract string that underlies this—cf. n. 2), with its derived phrase-marker. Call this new structure K_1. At this point, apply the generalized embedding transformation T_{Emb} to the pair of structures (B_2, K_1), deleting the occurrence of *the man* in the embedded sentence in the process, giving the string 'someone fired the man who quit work' with its derived phrase-marker K_2. To K_2, apply the passive transformation T_{Pass} to give 'the man who quit work was fired by someone', with the phrase-marker K_3. To this apply the deletion transformation T_{Del} to give 'the man who quit work was fired', with the derived phrase-marker K_4. Now apply to the pair of structures (B_1, K_4) the generalized embedding transformation T_{Emb}, giving 'I expected the man who quit work was fired' with the derived phrase-marker K_5. To K_5, apply the singulary transformation T_{to} giving the sentence (18) with its derived phrase-marker K_6.

[10] Since I am presenting this merely as the basis for some revisions to be proposed below, I skip many details. In particular, I am completely overlooking the question of how to describe the Auxiliary system, and I have also supposed, for simplicity of exposition, that each of B_1–B_3 underlies a kernel sentence. Actually, this is not necessary, and in the transformational grammars presented in Chomsky, 'The Logical Structure of Linguistic Theory', *Syntactic Structures*, 'A Transformational Approach to Syntax', Lees, *The Grammar of English Nominalizations*, and others, many of the base strings contain 'dummy symbols' (e.g. *Comp*, in the case of the analysis of such sentences as (15)) which are either deleted or filled in by sentence transforms in one way or another. Thus B_1 might have a dummy symbol as Object, B_2 might have an unspecified Subject, etc.

I am also assuming here a simpler analysis of the main (matrix) structure than was postulated in earlier work. The reasons for this go well beyond anything considered here. See P. Rosenbaum, 'A Grammar of English Predicate Complement Constructions', unpublished Ph.D. dissertation (M.I.T., 1965), and, for further related discussion, Chomsky, *Aspects of the Theory of Syntax*, Ch, 1, § 4.

Throughout the description of these structures, I cite sentences as examples, inaccurately, instead of the abstract strings that underlie them. It should be kept in mind that this is only an expository device.

I emphasize once again that only after all the transformations have been completed do we have an actual 'sentence'—that is, a string of elements that constitutes an 'output' of the syntactic component of the grammar and an 'input' to the phonological component.

Perhaps this example suffices to convey the content of the notion 'T-marker' (for further elaboration, see Chomsky, 'The Logical Structure of Linguistic Theory'; Katz and Postal, *An Integrated Theory of Linguistic Description*). It should be clear, from this, how any transformational derivation can be presented as a T-marker which gives the full 'transformational history' of the derived sentence, including, in particular, a specification of the base phrase-markers from which it is derived. In Chomsky, 'The Logical Structure of Linguistic Theory', a general theory of linguistic levels is developed in an abstract and uniform way, with phrase structure and transformations each constituting a linguistic level. On each level, markers are constructed that represent a sentence. In particular, derived phrase-markers and T-markers fill this function on the phrase-structure and transformational levels, respectively. Each level is a system of representation in terms of certain primes (elementary atomic symbols of this level). On the level of phrase structure, the primes are category and terminal symbols. On the level of transformations, the primes are base phrase-markers and transformations. A marker is a string of primes or a set of such strings. Both phrase-markers and transformation-markers can be represented in this way. Levels are organized in a hierarchy, and we may think of the markers of each level as being mapped into the markers of the next lowest level and as representing the lowest level marker (that is, the phonetic representation which is the marker on the lowest, phonetic level—the primes of this level being sets of features), which is associated directly with an actual signal. We limit the discussion here to the levels of phrase structure and transformational structure.

The general requirement on a syntactic theory is that it define the notions 'deep structure' and 'surface structure', representing the inputs to the semantic and phonological components of a grammar respectively (see above), and state precisely how a syntactic description consisting of a deep and surface structure is generated by the syntactic rules. These requirements are met by the theory outlined above in the following way. The rewriting rules of the base component and the rules governing ordering and arrangement of transformations generate an infinite class of T-markers, in the manner just sketched. We take a T-marker to be the deep structure; we take the derived phrase-marker that is the final output of the operations represented in the T-marker to be the surface structure. Thus in the case of (18), the deep structure is the T-marker represented as (19), and the surface structure is what we designated as K_6. The phrase-marker K_6, then, must contain all information relevant to determination of the form of the signal corresponding to (18) (i.e. it is to be mapped into a phonetic representation of (18) by rules of the phonological component); the T-marker (19) is to contain all information relevant to the semantic interpretation of (18).

To complete the theory, we must add a description of the phonological and semantic components that interpret surface and deep structures, respectively. I will discuss the phonological component briefly in the fourth section, along lines suggested by R. Jakobson, G. Fant and M. Halle, *Preliminaries to Speech Analysis* (Cambridge, Mass., 1952); Chomsky, Halle and Lukoff, 'On Accent and Juncture in English'; Halle, *The Sound Pattern of Russian,* 'Phonology in a Generative Grammar', 'On the Bases of Phonology' (*Structure of Language,* eds. Fodor and Katz, pp. 324–33); Chomsky, 'Explanatory Models in Linguistics'; and other related publications. The theory of semantic interpretation is in a much less developed state, as noted above, although recent work of Katz, Fodor and Postal has been quite encouraging and, as we shall note directly, has had important consequences for the theory of syntax as well.

A theory of semantic interpretation based on the syntactic model outlined above would have to provide, first, a characterization of the notion 'semantic interpretation of a sentence', and second, a system of rules for assigning such an object to a deep structure, that is, a T-marker. Analogously a theory of phonetic interpretation must specify the notion 'phonetic interpretation of a sentence'—it must, in other words, specify a universal phonetic alphabet—and must provide a system of rules for assigning such an object to a surface structure, that is, the final derived phrase-marker of a sentence. The notion 'semantic interpretation of a sentence' remains in a rather primitive state, for the moment. Several important steps have been taken towards the study of rules that assign semantic interpretations to deep structures, however.

First of all, it is evident that the grammatical relations among the elements of the string representing a sentence and the grammatical functions (i.e. Subject, Object, etc.) that these elements fulfil provide information that is fundamental for semantic interpretation. Furthermore, it has been evident since the beginnings of recent work on transformational grammar that it is the grammatical relations and grammatical functions represented in the base phrase-markers underlying a sentence that are critical for its semantic interpretation (for example, it is not the 'grammatical subject' of the passive but rather its 'logical subject' that is the subject in the sense relevant to semantic interpretation). This is evident from consideration of the examples discussed throughout this paper. These examples were chosen primarily to illustrate this fact, as is characteristic of expository papers in transformational grammar. As emphasized above, it is examples of grammatical relations and functions that are obscured in the surface representation (the IC analysis) that provide the primary motivation for the rejection of all versions of taxonomic syntax, and for the development of the theory of transformational grammar.

To my knowledge, the first fairly explicit discussion of grammatical relations of the deep structure that are not represented in the actual physical form and organization of the sentence, and the first general discussion of the importance of these for semantic interpretation, is in the *Grammaire générale et raisonnée* of Port-Royal (1660).

For some brief references, see Chomsky, *Current Issues in Linguistic Theory*, § 1, and for some further discussion, Chomsky, *Cartesian Linguistics*. In modern linguistics, the same insight was expressed by Harris, in somewhat different terms, in his early work on transformations,[11] and the point is also emphasized in Chomsky, 'The Logical Structure of Linguistic Theory', *Syntactic Structures*, and in all subsequent work on transformational grammar.

To go beyond this observation, it is necessary to define grammatical relations and grammatical functions, and to show how the relations and functions of the base phrase-markers play a role in determining the semantic interpretation of the sentence that they underlie. A phrase-structure grammar is, in fact, a very natural device for assigning a system of grammatical relations and functions to a generated string. These notions are represented directly in the phrase-marker assigned to a string generated by such rules, as has been frequently pointed out. Various ways of defining these notions are discussed in Chomsky ('The Logical Structure of Linguistic Theory'; *Current Issues in Linguistic Theory*; *Aspects of the Theory of Syntax*) and Postal (*Constituent Structure*). For concreteness, consider a highly oversimplified phrase-structure grammar with the rules (21):

(21)
$$S \rightarrow NP\ VP$$
$$VP \rightarrow V\ NP$$
$$NP \rightarrow John,\ Bill$$
$$V \rightarrow saw$$

This grammar generates the string 'John saw Bill' with the phrase-marker (22):

(22)

To the grammatical rule $A \rightarrow XBY$, we can associate the *grammatical function* [B, A]. Thus associated with the rules of (21) we have the grammatical functions [NP, S], [VP, S], [V, VP], [NP, VP]. We may give these the conventional names *Subject-of*, *Predicate-of*, *Main-Verb-of*, *Object-of*, respectively. Using the obvious definitions of these notions, we can say, then, that with respect to the phrase-marker (22), *John* is the Subject-of the sentence, *saw Bill* is the Predicate-of the sentence, *saw* is the Main-Verb-of the Verb Phrase, and *Bill* is the Object-of the Verb Phrase. We can go on to define grammatical relations (Subject-Verb, etc.) in terms of these and other notions

---

[11] e.g. Harris, 'Discourse Analysis', *Lg.*, 28, pp. 18–23 (1952); 'Distributional Structure', *Word*, 10, pp. 146–62 (1954); 'Co-occurrence and Transformation in Linguistic Structure', *Lg.*, 33, pp. 283–340 (1957).

and there are various ways in which one can attempt to formulate language-independent definitions for the central concepts (for details, see the cited references). The important point is that a phrase-structure grammar need not be supplemented in any way for it to assign these properties to the strings it generates. Once we recognize the relational character of these notions, we see at once they are already assigned, in the appropriate way, with no further elaboration of the rules.

Notice that we might define the grammatical functions not in terms of the generating rules, but in terms of the phrase-marker itself, in an obvious way. If we do this, we will have a more general notion of 'grammatical function' that will apply to derived phrase-markers as well as to the base phrase-markers. I do not go into this here, since, in any event, it is only the functions in the base phrase-markers that are significant for semantic interpretation (but see Chomsky, *Aspects of the Theory of Syntax*, pp. 220, 221, for some discussion of the role of 'surface functions', so defined).

The first attempt to develop a theory of semantic interpretation as an integral part of an explicit (i.e. generative) grammar is in Katz and Fodor, ('The Structure of a Semantic Theory'). This is the first study that goes beyond the assertion that the base phrase-markers underlying a sentence are, in some sense, the basic content elements that determine its semantic interpretation. Basing themselves on the account of syntactic structure outlined above, Katz and Fodor argue that the semantic component of a grammar should be a purely interpretive system of rules that maps a deep structure (a T-marker) into a semantic interpretation, utilizing in the process three sorts of information: (i) intrinsic semantic features of lexical items; (ii) the grammatical functions defined by the base rules; (iii) the structure of the T-marker. The semantic component should have two sorts of 'projection rules'. The first type assign semantic interpretations ('readings') to categories of the base phrase-markers in terms of the readings previously assigned to the elements dominated by (belonging to) these categories, beginning with the intrinsic readings of the lexical items and using the grammatical functions defined by the configurations of the base phrase-markers to determine how the higher level readings are assigned; and, ultimately, assigning a reading to the dominant category S. The projection rules of the second type utilize the readings assigned in this way to base phrase-markers, and, in terms of the elements and configurations represented in the T-marker, determine the semantic interpretation of the full sentence. Not much is said about type two rules; as we shall see below, this is not a serious gap in their theory.

With this brief survey, we conclude part three of the outline of the introductory section, having now sketched a certain theory of generative grammar that in part overcomes the fundamental inability of taxonomic syntax to provide an adequate notion of deep structure.

Turning now to part four of the outline, I would like to consider some of the defects that have been exposed in the theory just sketched as it has been applied to linguistic material.

In Lees, *The Grammar of English Nominalizations*, it is shown that the negation transformation of Chomsky (*Syntactic Structures*, 'A Transformational Approach to Syntax')[12] is incorrectly formulated. He shows that there are syntactic arguments in favour of an alternative formulation in which the negation element is not introduced by a transformation but is, rather, an optional element introduced by rewriting rules of the base, the transformation serving simply to place it in the correct position in the sentence. At about the same time, E. S. Klima pointed out that the same is true of the question transformations of Chomsky, *Syntactic Structures*, 'A Transformational Approach to Syntax'. There are syntactic arguments in favour of assuming an abstract 'question marker' as an element introduced by base rules, the question transformations then being conditional on the presence of this marker (i.e. obligatory when it appears in a string, and inapplicable otherwise). Further arguments in support of this view, and further elaboration of it, are presented in Katz and Postal, *An Integrated Theory of Linguistic Description*. See now also Klima, 'Negation in English', *Structure of Language: Readings in the Philosophy of Language*, eds. Fodor and Katz, pp. 246–323.

In Katz and Postal, it is further observed that the same is true of the imperative transformation of earlier work. In the light of this and other observations, Katz and Postal then conclude that all singulary transformations which affect meaning are conditional upon the presence of markers of this sort; in other words, the singulary transformations in themselves need not be referred to by the rules of the semantic component since whatever contribution they appear to make to the meaning of the sentence can be regarded as an intrinsic property of the marker that determines their applicability, and can therefore be handled in base structures by type 1 projection rules. It follows, then, that the function of type 2 projection rules is much more restricted than Katz and Fodor were forced to assume, since they need not take into account the presence of singulary transformations in a T-marker.

Turning then to generalized transformations, Katz and Postal carry out a detailed analysis of many examples described in earlier studies that seem to demonstrate a contribution of generalized transformations to the semantic interpretation of the generated sentence in some way that goes beyond mere 'amalgamation'. They argue (quite convincingly, it seems to me) that in each such case, there are syntactic grounds for regarding the description as in error; furthermore, that in each such case the only function of the generalized transformation is to embed a sentence transform in a position that is already in the underlying structure (let us say, by the presence of a dummy symbol).

Generalizing upon these various observations, they conclude that the only function of generalized transformations, so far as semantic interpretation is concerned, is to interrelate the semantic interpretations of the phrase-markers on which they operate; in other words, to insert the reading for the embedded phrase-marker in the position

[12] Publication delays account for the discrepancy in dates, here, and in several other places.

already marked (by a dummy element) in the phrase-marker in which it is inserted. Thus the only aspect of the T-marker that need be considered in semantic interpretation is the interrelation specified by the nodes where generalized transformations appear in the representation. Beyond this, transformations appear to play no role in semantic interpretation. Thus the function of type 2 rules is still further restricted.

This principle obviously simplifies very considerably the theory of the semantic component as this was presented in Katz and Fodor, 'The Structure of a Semantic Theory'. It is therefore important to observe that there is no question-begging in the Katz–Postal argument. That is, the justification for the principle is not that it simplifies semantic theory, but rather that in each case in which it was apparently violated, syntactic arguments can be produced to show that the analysis was in error on internal, syntactic grounds. In the light of this observation, it is reasonable to formulate the principle tentatively as a general property of grammar.

Furthermore, it seems that there are good reasons for regarding even the passive transformation as conditional upon the presence of an abstract marker in the underlying string (see Chomsky, *Aspects of the Theory of Syntax*, for a survey of syntactic arguments in support of this), rather than as optional, as assumed in earlier work. Consequently, it seems that all singular transformations other than those that are 'purely stylistic' (cf. Chomsky, *Aspects of the Theory of Syntax*, pp. 221, 223, for some discussion of this distinction—discussion, incidentally, which is far from satisfactory, although it seems to me that a real and important distinction is involved) are conditional upon markers in base strings, whether or not these transformations effect semantic interpretation.

Independently of these developments, C. J. Fillmore pointed out that there are many restrictions on the organization of T-markers beyond those that were assumed in earlier attempts to formulate a theory of transformational grammar (Fillmore, 'The Position of Embedding Transformations in a Grammar', *Word*, pp. 19, 208–31 (1963)). What his observations come to is essentially this: there is no ordering among generalized transformations, although singular transformations are ordered (apparently linearly); there are no singular transformations that must apply to a matrix sentence before a constituent sentence is embedded in it by a generalized embedding transformation,[13] although there are many instances of singular transformations that must apply to a matrix sentence after embedding of a constituent structure within it and to a constituent sentence before it is embedded; embedding

---

[13] The terms 'matrix sentence' and 'constituent sentence' are due to Lees, *The Grammar of English Nominalizations*; the matrix sentence is the one into which a constituent sentence is inserted by a generalized transformation. The same notion appears in the analysis of transformational processes in the *Grammaire générale et raisonnée*, where the terms 'proposition essentielle' and 'proposition incidente' are used for 'matrix sentence' and 'constituent sentence', respectively. Actually 'matrix proposition' and 'constituent proposition' would, in any event, be preferable terms, since what is involved here is not an operation on sentences but rather on the abstract structures that underlie them and determine their semantic interpretation. This is the way in which these operations are interpreted, correctly, in the *Grammaire générale et raisonnée*.

should be regarded as substitution of a sentence transform for a 'dummy symbol' rather than as insertion of this transform in a categorially unspecified position. The last observation is further elaborated by Katz and Postal, *An Integrated Theory of Linguistic Description*, as noted above.

Returning now to the T-marker (19) used as an example above, we observe that it has just the properties that Fillmore outlines. That is, singulary transformations are applied to a matrix sentence only after embedding and the only ordering is among singularies. But the earlier theory of T-markers left open the possibility for ordering of a much more complex sort. It is therefore quite natural to generalize from these empirical observations, and to propose as a general condition on T-markers that they must always meet Fillmore's conditions and have the form illustrated in (19).

As just formulated, this principle appears to be quite *ad hoc*, but there is another way of saying exactly the same thing that makes it seem entirely natural. Notice that if no singulary transformations apply to a matrix phrase-marker before embedding, and if, furthermore, all embedding involves the insertion of a constituent phrase-marker in a position marked by a dummy element in the matrix structure, then we can, in fact, dispense with generalized transformations entirely. Instead of introducing constituent phrase-markers by embedding transformations, we can permit the rewriting rules of the base to introduce the initial category symbol S, i.e. we can permit rewriting rules of the form $A \rightarrow \ldots S \ldots$

Wherever such a symbol is introduced, we can allow it to head a new base derivation. In short, we can apply the linearly ordered system of base rewriting rules in a cyclic fashion, returning to the beginning of the sequence each time we come upon a new occurrence of S introduced by a rewriting rule. Proceeding in this way, we construct what we can call a *generalized phrase-marker*.

We now apply the linear sequence of singulary transformations in the following manner. First, apply the sequence to the most deeply embedded structure dominated by S in the generalized phrase-marker. Having completed the application of the rules to each such structure, reapply the sequence to the 'next-higher' structure dominated by S in the generalized phrase-marker. Continue in this way, until, finally, the sequence of transformations is applied to the structure dominated by the occurrence of S which initiated the first application of base rules, i.e. to the generalized phrase-marker as a whole. Notice that with this formulation, we have, in effect, established the particular formal properties of the T-marker (19) as general properties of any transformational derivation.

Let us now return to the example (18)–(20) in the light of these suggested revisions of the theory of transformational grammar. By the application of the rewriting rules of the base, we construct the generalized phrase-marker (23) (omitting all but the central configurations, and many details).

The transformations indicated in (19) now apply, obligatorily, in the following order. First, T_{Rel} applies to the most deeply embedded structure. We then turn to the next higher structure, i.e. the one dominated by the occurrence of S in the fourth line of (23). At this point, an inversion rule (not indicated in (19), though in fact also needed in the earlier formulation) inverts the relative clause and the following N. Next we apply the passive transformation and the subsequent deletion of the unspecified subject, these operations now being obligatorily marked by the dummy elements passive and $\triangle$ (standing for an unspecified category) in (23). Since no further transformational rules apply at this point, we turn to the next higher structure dominated by S—in this case, the full generalized phrase-marker. To this we apply T_{to}, as before, giving (18). The transformations indicated in the T-marker (19) are now obligatory and the structure of the T-marker (19) is fully determined by (23) itself, given the general convention for cyclic application of transformations.

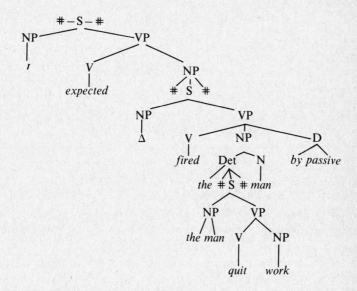

Notice now that all of the information to the semantic interpretation of (18) is contained in the generalized phrase-marker (23) that underlies (18). Furthermore, the same will be true in all other cases, if the modifications suggested above are correct. By the principle suggested by Katz and Postal, the singulary transformations will not make an intrinsic contribution to meaning, and the generalized transformations will do so only in so far as they interrelate base phrase-markers. But we have now eliminated generalized transformations in favour of a recursive operation in the base. Consequently all information relevant to the operation of the interpretive semantic component should be contained in the generalized phrase-marker generated by base rules.

The advantages of this modification are obvious. It provides a more highly structured theory which is weaker in expressive power; in other words, it excludes in principle certain kinds of derivational pattern that were permitted by the earlier version of transformational theory, but never actually found. Since the primary goal of linguistic theory is to account for specific properties of particular languages in terms of hypotheses about language structure in general, any such strengthening of the constraints on a general theory is an important advance. Furthermore, there is good internal motivation for enriching the structure (and hence decreasing the expressive power) of transformational theory in this way, namely, in that this modification permits us to eliminate the notion of 'generalized transformation' (and with it, the notion 'T-marker') from the theory of syntax. Hence the theory is conceptually simpler. Finally, the theory of the semantic component can be simplified in that type 2 projection rules are no longer necessary at all.

Recapitulating, we are proposing that the syntactic component of a grammar consists of rewriting rules and transformational rules. The rewriting rules are permitted to introduce the initial symbol S. These rules apply in a linear sequence; if the initial symbol S appears in a derivation, then the sequence of rules reapplies to form a subderivation dominated by this symbol, in the usual manner. The recursive property of the grammar (its 'creative aspect', to return to terminology used above) is restricted to the base component. In fact, the restriction may be still heavier than this, since recursion may be limited to introduction of the symbol S, that is, to introduction of 'propositional content'. This is not a necessary property of a phrase-structure grammar.

The base rules, applying in the way just outlined, form generalized phrase-markers. The function of the transformational rules is to map generalized phrase-markers into derived phrase-markers. If the transformational rules map the generalized phrase-marker M_D into the final derived phrase-marker M_S of the sentence X, then M_D is the deep structure of X and M_S is its surface structure.

This approach to syntax formalizes, in one specific way, the view that the phonetic form of a sentence is determined by its actual labelled bracketing, whereas its semantic interpretation is determined by the intrinsic semantic properties of its lexical items and by a network of grammatical relations, not necessarily represented in the surface structure, that interconnect these items (cf. (13)). The underlying grammatical relations are determined by the base rules. This abstract system of categories and relations is related to a labelled bracketing of the actual sentence by transformational rules and the interpretive rules of the phonological component. There is fairly good reason to suppose that the base rules are rather narrowly constrained both in terms of the symbols that may appear in them and in terms of the configurations of these symbols, but I will not go into this further question here (see Chomsky, *Aspects of the Theory of Syntax*, for some discussion). In so far as information is presently available about syntactic structure, and about the relation of signals to semantic interpretations of these signals, this view seems compatible with it. It is worth mentioning that a view very much like this is expressed in the *Grammaire générale et raisonnée*, to which we have now had occasion to refer several times.

We might ask why a natural language should be constructed in this way; why, in particular, should it not identify deep and surface structures and thus dispense with the transformations that interrelate them. One would naturally attempt to find an answer to this question on perceptual grounds. For some speculations that seem to me worth pursuing further, see Miller and Chomsky, 'Finitary Models of Language Users', part II.

Observe that the base rules may form generalized phrase-markers that cannot be mapped by any sequence of transformations into a surface structure. For example, suppose that we had chosen the phrase 'the boy' instead of 'the man' in the most deeply embedded structure of (23). In this case, the generalized phrase-marker would evidently constitute the deep structure of no sentence; there is no sentence for which this structure provides the semantic interpretation. And in fact, the relative transformation would block when applying to this structure, because of the lack of identity between the Noun Phrases of the matrix and constituent sentences.[14] Hence not all generalized phrase-markers underlie sentences and thus count as deep structures. The deep structures are the generalized phrase-markers that are mapped into well-formed surface structures by transformational rules. Thus the transformations serve a 'filtering' function; in effect, they supply certain global constraints that a deep structure must meet, constraints that are, in fact, entirely unstatable within the framework of elementary rewriting rules that seem perfectly adequate for the generation of base structures with the grammatical functions and relations that they express. For further discussion of this property of transformations, see Chomsky, *Aspects of the Theory of Syntax*, Ch. 3.

In this way, we can construct a theory of grammatical transformations that is conceptually simpler than the earlier version, described above, but still apparently empirically adequate. In this modified formulation, the functions of the base rules and the transformational rules are more clearly expressed, as are also the notions of deep and surface structure. We have, correspondingly, a simplification of semantic theory.[15]

I began this section by presenting a certain theory of grammar in outline. I have now tried to show that this theory was too broad and rich in expressive power, and that a much more restricted version of it (which is, furthermore, conceptually well motivated) will suffice to account for what empirical data are now available. I would

[14] What is involved here is a set of very general conventions on recoverability of deletion, in the transformational component of a grammar. For discussion, see Chomsky, *Current Issues in Linguistic Theory*; *Aspects of the Theory of Syntax*; Katz and Postal, *An Integrated Theory of Linguistic Description.*

[15] Incidentally, only embedding transformations were considered here. It is also necessary to show how various transformations that introduce coordinate structures (e.g. conjunction) can be developed within this framework. For some remarks on this question, see Chomsky, *Aspects of the Theory of Syntax*, and the references cited there.

now like to turn to an inadequacy in earlier theory of the opposite sort, that is, to a class of problems that show this theory to be too poor in expressive power, in a certain way.

Let us limit our attention now to the base component of the syntax. The theory outlined followed structuralist assumptions in supposing that the relation of lexical items to the categories to which they belong is fundamentally the same as the relation of phrases to categories of which they are members. Formally speaking, it was assumed that lexical item X is introduced by rewriting rules of the form $A \rightarrow X$, where A is a lexical category, exactly in the way that phrases are introduced.[16] However, difficulties in this view quickly emerged. Shortly after the publication of the earliest work in transformational generative grammar, it was pointed out by G. H. Matthews that whereas the categorization of phrases is typically hierarchic, and therefore within the bounds of phrase-structure grammar, lexical categorization typically involves cross-classification, and therefore goes beyond these bounds. For example, a Noun may be either Proper or Common, and, independently of this, may be either Animate or Inanimate; a Verb may be Transitive or non-Transitive, and independently of this, may or may not take non-Animate Subjects; etc. This fact is unstatable within the framework of phrase structure grammar. Consequently, the theory of the base must be extended in some way so as to provide an analysis of lexical categorization that is different in fundamental respects from the analysis in terms of rewriting rules that seem quite adequate above the level of lexical category. Similar observations were made independently by Stockwell, Anderson, Schachter and Bach, and various proposals have been made as to how to remedy this defect of the base component. The general problem is studied in some detail in Chomsky, *Aspects of the Theory of Syntax*, Ch. 2, where reference is also made to the earlier work just noted. I will sketch briefly the proposals offered there for modification of the theory of the base component.

Notice that the problem of lexical cross-classification is formally analogous to the problem of phonological classification. Thus phonological elements are also typically cross-classified with respect to the operation of various phonological rules. Certain rules apply to the category of Voiced segments; others to the category of Continuents; membership of a segment in one of these categories is independent of its membership in the other. This is, furthermore, the typical situation. This, in fact, is one major reason for the view that segments (e.g. phonemes or morphophonemes) have no independent linguistic status and are simply to be regarded as sets of features.

More generally, a lexical item can be represented phonologically as a certain set of features, indexed as to position. Thus the lexical item *bee* can be represented by the

---

[16] Notice that although this has been the view of all work in modern syntactic theory that has gone beyond mere elaboration of terminology, the incorrectness of this view becomes obvious only when it was formalized within the framework of an explicit theory of grammar. An essential reason for formalization and explicitness is, of course, that it immediately exposes inadequacies that may otherwise be far from evident.

feature set [Consonantal$_1$, Voiced$_1$, non-Continuant$_1$, ..., Vocalic$_2$, non-Grave$_2$,...]
indicating that its first 'segment' is consonantal, voiced, a non-continuant, ..., and
that its second 'segment' is vocalic, non-grave, ... Such a representation can be
given in matrix form in an obvious and familiar way. It provides a perfectly satisfactory solution to the cross-classification problem on the phonological level (and
furthermore relates very nicely to what seems to me to be for the present the most
satisfactory theory of universal phonetics namely, Jakobson's theory of distinctive
features—I will presuppose acquaintance with this, in the form recently given it by
Halle, for the remainder of this paper).

Observe also that the semantic analysis of lexical items also apparently requires
a kind of feature theory, and that these features typically cross-classify lexical entries.
Thus Katz and Fodor, 'The Structure of a Semantic Theory', and Katz and Postal,
An Integrated Theory of Linguistic Description, are led to the conclusion, essentially,
that a lexical entry in its semantic aspect should consist of a set of semantic features.

These observations suggest that the problem of syntactic cross-classification be
dealt with in the same way, particularly, since it apparently involves only lexical
items and not phrase types. Adopting this rather natural proposal, let us revise the
theory of the base in the following way. The base consists of a system (presumably,
a linear sequence) of rewriting rules which we may call its *categorial component*.
Beyond this, it contains a *lexicon*. The lexicon is an unordered set of *lexical entries*.
Each lexical entry is simply a set of specified features. The features constituting the
lexical entry may be phonological (e.g. [$\pm$ Voiced$_n$], where n is an integer indicating
position), semantic (e.g. [$\pm$ Artifact]), or syntactic (e.g. [$\pm$ Proper]). We limit our
attention here to the syntactic features. The categorial component of the base
generates no lexical items in strings (though it may introduce grammatical morphemes). As a first approximation, we may think of each lexical category A (e.g.
Noun, Verb, etc.) as being involved only in rewriting rules of the form A $\rightarrow$ $\triangle$, where
$\triangle$ is a fixed dummy symbol. Thus the final strings generated by the categorial component (let us call these *pre-terminal strings*) are based on a 'vocabulary' (i.e. a set
of primes—see above, p. 86) consisting of grammatical morphemes and the
symbol $\triangle$. The latter will occupy the position in which items from the lexicon will
be inserted, in a manner which we will describe directly. A pre-terminal string is
converted to a *terminal string* by insertion of an appropriate lexical item in each
position marked by $\triangle$.

Recall that the deep structures that determine semantic interpretation are generalized phrase-markers generated by the base component. As we noted above, it seems
plausible to develop semantic theory in terms of projection rules that assign readings
to successively higher nodes of the deep structure, basing this assignment on the
readings assigned to already interpreted nodes and the grammatical relations represented by the configuration in question. The grammatical relations and the order of
application of the interpretive projection rules are determined completely by the

categorial component of the base. The intrinsic semantic properties that provide the initial readings for this process of semantic interpretation (i.e. the readings of the lexical items that are the terminal elements of the generalized phrase-marker) are provided completely by the lexicon. Thus the two separate aspects of the semantic theory are mirrored in the subdivision of the base into a categorial and a lexical component.

The functioning of the categorial component is clear; let us, therefore, consider the lexicon in some further detail. The lexical entry for a certain item should contain all information about idiosyncratic features of this lexical item, features that cannot be predicted by general rule. Thus the fact that 'buy' begins with a Voiced non-Continuant, that it is a transitive Verb, that it has irregular inflexions, that it involves transfer of ownership, etc., must all be represented by features of the lexical entry. Other properties (for example, that the intitial non-Continuant is non-Aspirated) can be predicted by rule (in this case, a phonological rule). But there may be *redundancy rules* of various kinds that operate on phonological, semantic, and syntactic features, and that specify interrelations among features of the various types. In so far as regularities concerning feature composition can be expressed by rule, the features in question can be extracted from the lexical entry (for discussion of redundancy rules, see Chomsky, *Aspects of the Theory of Syntax*, particularly Ch. 4, § 2.1). Normally, a lexical item will be idiosyncratic in many respects. Since these can now be specified in the lexical entry, they need no longer be represented in the rewriting rules. This leads to an enormous simplification of the base component, as will be evident to anyone who has ever attempted to construct a detailed grammatical description.

Let us now consider the rule that inserts lexical items in pre-terminal strings. Notice that this rule must take account of the structure of the phrase-marker in which the item is being inserted. For example, when we say that a Verb is Transitive, we are asserting that it can appear in the position—NP in a Verb Phrase. Therefore the syntactic feature [+Transitive] must specify some aspect of the phrase-marker in which the item can be inserted. Let us call a feature of this sort a *contextual Feature*. In contrast, we will call such features of Nouns as [±Human] *non-contextual*. The degenerate case of a contextual feature is the feature [±Noun] itself, which indicates a minimal aspect of the phrase-marker, namely, the category dominating the occurrence of △ for which the item in question may be substituted. These degenerate contextual features, we may call *category features*. For the category features, the obvious notation is [±A], where A is a lexical category. By convention, then, we assert that an item with the category feature [+A] can only replace an occurrence of △ dominated by the category symbol A.

Consider now the problem of a proper notation for the other contextual features, e.g. transitivity. Clearly the best notation is simply an indication of the context in which the item can occur. Thus the feature [+Transitive] can be represented simply [+ — NP]. Similarly, the fact that 'persuade' can be followed by a Noun Phrase and a following Prepositional Phrase (e.g. 'I persuaded John of the pointlessness of his actions') can be indicated by assigning the contextual feature [+ — NP PP] to the lexical entry for 'persuade' (in fact, this is apparently the only contextual feature needed to specify the frame in which 'persuade' can appear, all other forms being derived by transformation—for discussion, see Chomsky, *Aspects of the Theory of Syntax*). Contextual features of this sort, which specify the frame in which an item can be substituted, we will call *strict subcategorization features*.

Alongside of strict subcategorization features, there are contextual features of a radically different sort that we will call *selectional features*. Whereas the strict subcategorization features specify categorial frames in which an item may appear, the selectional features of a lexical item X specify lexical features of the items with which X enters into grammatical relations. Thus the selectional features for 'frighten' will indicate that its Object must be specified as [+ Animate], the selectional features for 'elapse' will indicate that its Subject cannot be [+ Human] (and for true descriptive adequacy, must obviously give a much narrower specification than this), etc. Similarly, the selectional features for 'abundant' must indicate that it can be predicated of 'harvest' but not 'boy', whereas the selectional features for 'clever' must contain the opposite specification. We can represent selectional features by a notation very much like that suggested above for strict subcategorization features.

Contextual features can be regarded as specifying certain substitution transformations. The context stated in the contextual feature specifies the condition that must be met by the phrase-marker to which the transformation in question applies and the manner in which this phrase-marker must be analysed for the purposes of this transformation. Thus it defines the structural analysis of the transformation (see above, p. 84. The elementary transformation that completes the definition of the transformation states that the lexical item in question (i.e. the set of specified features that constitutes the lexical entry) substitutes for the occurrence of △ that appears in the position indicated in the structural analysis.

It is clear from the examples that there are many restrictions on the form of the substitution transformations defined by contextual features. Thus the strict subcategorization features only involve 'local contexts'—i.e. contexts dominated by the phrase category that immediately dominates the lexical category for which the lexical item is substituted. On the other hand, selectional features refer only to 'heads' of grammatical related constructions. These restrictions can be made precise, and can be shown to lead to certain interesting consequences concerning the possible constraints that may appear in a grammar. For discussion, see again Chomsky, *Aspects of the Theory of Syntax*.

I have not discussed the problem of deviation from grammaticalness here. However, it is clear that whenever a grammatical rule exists, we may ask how a sentence is interpreted that deviates from this rule. It seems that sentences deviating from selectional rules are interpreted quite differently from those deviating from strict subcategorization rules. Deviation from selectional rules gives such examples as 'colourless green ideas sleep furiously', 'sincerity admires John', etc.; deviation from strict subcategorization rules gives such examples as 'John persuaded to leave', 'John found sad', etc. Sentences of the former type are often interpreted as somehow metaphorical; sentences of the latter type, if interpretable at all, must be looked at in an entirely different way. Deviations from contextual rules involving category features (see above, p. 98) are still different in interpretive potential. Thus the various types of contextual feature are rather different in the conditions that they impose on sentence structures.

Notice incidentally that the ease with which sentences deviating from selectional rules can be interpreted is not simply a result of the fact that 'low-level' syntactic features such as [± Human] or [takes Animate Object] are involved. These features can participate in rules that are not at all violable in the way in which selectional rules may be (consider, for example, such expressions as 'the table who I scratched with a knife', 'who I saw was John', 'a very barking dog', etc.). There is much to say about this general problem; it is clear, however, that a nontrivial study of it demands a rich and detailed understanding of the various types of grammatical process.

We assumed, in this brief account of syntactic features, that the features of a Noun are inherent to it and that the features that selectionally relate Nouns to Verbs or Nouns to Adjectives appear as contextual (selectional) features of the Verbs and Adjectives. This was not an arbitrary decision; it can easily be justified on syntactic grounds. For discussion of this question, and many of the other topics mentioned briefly here, see Chomsky, *Aspects of Theory of Syntax*, Ch. 2.

With this, I conclude part 5 of the introductory outline. I have now briefly sketched two major respects in which the first modern attempts to formulate a theory of grammatical transformations were shown to be defective by later work. The first defect was one of excessive richness in expressive power. We have now been discussing a defect of the opposite kind, namely, an inability to express certain aspects of grammatical structure, and have suggested a way to modify the theory so as to overcome this. The theory of transformational generative grammar that results from these modifications is conceptually quite simple, and is reasonably well supported by what empirical evidence is presently available. Each component of the theory has a well-defined function; I see no way in which any of the postulated mechanisms can be eliminated without sacrifice of descriptive adequacy, and know of no justification for postulating a more complex structure and organization of the theory of the syntactic component than what has been sketched in outline here. For the present, then, this theory seems to me to constitute the most satisfactory hypothesis as to the form of the syntactic component of a grammar.

VI

THE PHILOSOPHICAL RELEVANCE OF LINGUISTIC THEORY[1]

JERROLD J. KATZ

1. INTRODUCTION

THIS paper defends the relevance of linguistics to philosophy on the grounds that linguistic theory incorporates solutions to significant philosophical problems. The particular thesis to be defended here is that certain philosophical problems can be represented correctly as questions about the nature of language, and that, so represented, they can be solved on the basis of theoretical constructions that appear in linguistic theory.[2]

Synchronic linguistics involves two distinct but interrelated studies: a study of the diversity in forms of linguistic communication and a study of the limits of such diversity. In the former, linguists investigate what is unique about individual natural languages and formulate such facts in what are called *linguistic descriptions* (or *generative grammars*). In the latter, linguists investigate what is common to all natural languages and formulate these more general facts about language in *linguistic theory*. Linguistic theory, therefore, is a specification of the universals of language. Given this notion of linguistic theory, the thesis of this paper asserts that theoretical constructions initially devised by linguists to enable linguistic theory to systematically state uniformities across natural languages also fulfil the conditions on solutions to certain philosophical problems, owing to the nature of those problems. This thesis should not be interpreted as asserting that the linguist's descriptions of natural languages reveal philosophical insights that somehow must escape philosophers looking at the same languages. This thesis does not concern either a philosopher's

From *The Linguistic Turn*, ed. Richard Rorty (University of Chicago Press, 1967), pp. 340–55. © 1967 by the University of Chicago. All rights reserved. Reprinted by permission of the author and the University of Chicago Press.

[1] This paper is a revised and expanded version of my paper 'The Relevance of Linguistics to Philosophy', *The Journal of Philosophy*. This work was supported by a grant from the National Institute of Health, No. MH-05120-04, to Harvard University, Center for Cognitive Studies. It was also supported in part by the Joint Services Electronics Program (Contract DA 36-039-AMC-03200(E)); and in part by the U.S. Air Force (Contract AF 19 (628)-2487), National Science Foundation (Grant GP-2495), The National Institutes of Health (Grant MH-04737-05), and the National Aeronautics and Space Administration (Grant Ns G-496).

[2] In the final section of this paper, I will indicate another sort of relevance of linguistic theory to philosophy.

or a linguist's account of the facts about a natural language, but rather concerns the more abstract matters that are dealt with in an account of the facts about language in general.

If the defence of this thesis is successful, then linguistics is not incidentally pertinent to philosophy, in the way that philosophy of science bears upon the clarification of methodology and theory construction in linguistics, but is directly relevant in the same way that philosophical theories themselves are. Since I have no *a priori* notions about the *a priori* character of philosophical investigations, I am in no way disturbed by the fact that we might have to know quite a lot about extra-logical matters in order to solve certain philosophical problems.

Within the confines of a paper of this sort it is, of course, impossible to present all the arguments on behalf of this thesis, nor is it possible to formulate those that are presented in their full form. The present paper, then, is best regarded as a presentation of the thesis itself, with a sketch of some of the arguments that can be given for it.

2. THE RATIONALE FOR APPEALING TO LINGUISTICS

At the outset, it is appropriate to ask why an appeal to linguistics is necessary; why, that is, we find it necessary to go outside the boundaries of contemporary philosophy to search for the solutions to philosophical problems. The answer is simply that the approaches to the philosophical problems concerned that are available in contemporary philosophy have not dealt successfully with these problems and, moreover, that these approaches contain inherent difficulties which make it quite unlikely that they can deal successfully with them. In other publications, particularly 'What's Wrong with the Philosophy of Language?' and *The Philosophy of Language*,[3] I tried to show in some detail why the two major approaches in contemporary philosophy, Logical Empiricism (Logical Positivism) and Ordinary Language Philosophy, are inherently incapable of providing adequate, well-motivated solutions to the major philosophical problems they tackled. It is neither necessary nor possible to repeat my criticisms here. The general character of the difficulties, however, is this. Logical empiricism confined its efforts to the construction of highly arbitrary and conceptually impoverished theories about a class of artificial languages whose structure bears little similarity to that of natural languages. Ordinary language philosophy preoccupied itself with unearthing the most minute and detailed facts about the use of English locutions to the almost complete neglect of any concern with theory. Thus, while the former offered us philosophically irrelevant theories, the latter failed to give us any theory. Of course, both approaches prided themselves on their shortcomings, turning their vices into alleged virtues. Logical empiricism prided itself on its ex-

---

[3] J. J. Katz and J. A. Fodor, 'What's Wrong with the Philosophy of Language?' *Inquiry*, V (1962), pp. 197–237, and J. J. Katz, *The Philosophy of Language* (Harper & Row, New York, 1966).

clusive concern with artificial languages, claiming that natural languages are too irregular, amorphous, and vague to provide a basis for the solution to philosophical problems. Ordinary language philosophy prided itself on its avoidance of theory construction, claiming that theories cause the very philosophical perplexities that philosophy seeks to resolve by examination of the use of particular linguistic constructions. But the claim of the logical empiricists was never submitted to empirical investigations, nor, on the other hand, did logical empiricism provide an alternative standard for justifying a theory of artificial languages that might serve as a replacement for the standard of conformity to the facts of language that had been eliminated. Ordinary language philosophers never established that the theories in which they located the source of certain philosophical problems were not just bad theories, and so never seriously asked what a good theory would be able to do toward supplying a conceptual systematization of the facts of language that might offer solutions for the philosophical problems that arise in the course of ordinary, theoretically unsophisticated, uses of language. Accordingly, the solutions that these approaches presented were based either on unmotivated, and hence arbitrary, principles or on particularistic analyses of locutions whose bearing on philosophical problems were neither established nor made fully clear.

This unsatisfactory situation led a number of philosophers—with Quine as the most notable example—to turn some of their attention to empirical linguistics. Though, of course, I endorse this concern, I differ with them on a number of fundamental points. One is the question of what it is in linguistics for which philosophical relevance ought to be claimed, and another is the nature and extent of the relevance of linguistics to philosophy.

3. LINGUISTIC THEORY

I have claimed that the part of linguistics that is relevant to philosophy is linguistic theory. In this section, I will try to explain what this part of linguistics is.

As mentioned above, linguistic theory is a specification of the universals of language, the principles of organization and interpretation that are invariant from natural language to natural language. Linguistic theory expresses such invariants in the form of a model of a linguistic description, of which each empirically successful linguistic description must be an instance, exemplifying every aspect of the model. particular linguistic descriptions account for the diverse ways in which different natural languages realize the abstract structural pattern displayed in the model, while the model itself describes the form of a system of empirical generalizations capable of expressing and organizing the facts about a natural language.

Accordingly, the construction of linguistic theory and linguistic descriptions are strongly interdependent. Linguists can abstract out the common features from a set of linguistic descriptions and so generalize from them to hypotheses about linguistic universals. Alternatively, linguists can facilitate their task of describing a language by using the model provided by linguistic theory as a pattern for their systematization of the facts they uncover in field work. As a consequence, the justification of both linguistic theory and individual linguistic descriptions have a common basis, viz. the facts from natural languages on which linguistic descriptions depend for their empirical support. Since putative linguistic universals are inductively extrapolated generalizations, projected from known regularities cutting across the set of already constructed linguistic descriptions, their empirical adequacy is thus a matter of whether further facts, upon which newly constructed linguistic descriptions will eventually be based, continue to support these generalizations. Thus, the same facts that confirm or disconfirm particular linguistic descriptions also confirm or disconfirm a linguistic theory. Notice, finally, that if the general form of a particular linguistic description can be deduced from linguistic theory, then that linguistic description will be far better confirmed than were it to derive its support solely from the facts about the language it describes, since it will also be supported by a wealth of evidence from many natural languages via the connection through linguistic theory between their linguistic descriptions and this one.

Linguistic theory consists of three sub-theories, each corresponding to one of the three components of a linguistic description. The terms 'phonological theory', 'syntactic theory', and 'semantic theory' refer to these sub-theories, and 'phonological component', 'syntactic component', and 'semantic component' refer to the corresponding parts of a linguistic description. The phonological, syntactic, and semantic components are rule-formed descriptions of knowledge that a speaker has acquired in attaining fluency. The first states the rules determining the phonetic structure of speech sounds in a language; the second states the rules determining how speech sounds with a fixed phonetic shape are organized into sentential structures; the third states the rules determining how such sentential structures are interpreted as meaningful messages. At the level of linguistic theory, phonological, syntactic, and semantic theory, jointly, characterize the form of the rules in a linguistic description, specify the theoretical constructs utilized in writing actual rules in appropriate forms, and determine the relations between rules within each component.

Linguistic theory also specifies the relations between these components that weld them into an integrated linguistic description. The fundamental problem to which a linguistic description addresses itself is that of explicating the common system of rules on the basis of which different speakers of the same language can correlate the same speech signal with the same meaningful message. The ability of speakers to transmit their thoughts and ideas to one another through the vehicle of articulated speech sounds presupposes that each speaker has mastered a common system of rules within which each well-formed utterance receives a fixed semantic interpretation. Linguistic communication takes place when the same associations between sounds and meaning are made by different speakers in verbal interaction. Since the linguistic description must formally simulate the sound-meaning correlations made by speakers, its components must be related to one another in such a manner that the representations given by the phonological and syntactic components of the phonetic and syntactic character of a sentence are formally connected with the representation given by the semantic component of its meaning. The model of a linguistic description offered by linguistic theory must show that the various schemes for making such correlations that are found in different natural languages are instances of a general formula which is the same for all natural languages.

On the current model of a linguistic description,[4] this formula is embodied in the following organizational pattern for linguistic descriptions. The syntactic component is the generative source of the linguistic description. It generates abstract formal objects which are the input to the phonological and semantic components. Their outputs are, respectively, phonetic representations and semantic interpretations. Both these components are, therefore, purely interpretive systems. The output of the syntactic component is a syntactic description of each sentence of the language which consists of a set of *phrase-markers*, where a phrase-marker can be thought of as a labelled bracketing of the constituents of a sentence. The bracketing tells us that the elements enclosed within a single bracket form a constituent and the labelling tells us the syntactic category to which the constituent belongs. Thus, two words, phrases, or clauses are constituents of the same type if and only if they receive the same label. Now, the set of phrase-markers which constitutes the syntactic description of a sentence consists of a subset of *underlying phrase-markers* and a single *superficial phrase-marker*; the number of underlying phrase-markers in the syntactic description of a sentence indicates its degree of syntactic ambiguity (so that each underlying phrase-marker represents a syntactical unique sentence). An underlying phrase-marker describes that aspect of the syntax of a sentence of which its meaning is a function, while a superficial phrase-marker describes that aspect which determines its phonetic shape. Accordingly, the rules of the semantic component operate on the underlying phrase-markers of a sentence to provide its semantic interpretations, and the rules of the phonological component operate on the superficial phrase-marker to provide its phonetic representation. The underlying phrase-markers in a syntactic description are related to the superficial phrase-marker by virtue of the fact that this same superficial phrase-marker is transformationally derived from each of them. That is, transformations are syntactic rules that generate superficial phrase-markers from underlying phrase-markers. Thus, the set of underlying phrase-markers in a given syntactic description is automatically connected with the superficial phrase-marker in that description because the latter is obtained from each of the former by a specifiable (but in each case different) sequence of transformations and this

---

[4] Cf. J. J. Katz and P. Postal, *An Integrated Theory of Linguistic Descriptions* (Massachusetts Institute of Technology Press, Cambridge, 1964) and N. Chomsky, *Aspects of the Theory of Syntax* (Massachusetts Institute of Technology Press, Cambridge, 1965).

superficial phrase-marker is not transformationally obtainable from any underlying phrase-marker outside this set. Thus, the linguistic description will correlate the phonetic representation of a sentence with its semantic interpretation as desired, the correlation being effected by the transformations in the syntactic component and the manner in which the phonological and semantic components are organized to operate, respectively, on a superficial phrase-marker and the underlying phrase-marker from which it was transformationally derived.

4. ADVANTAGES OF LINGUISTIC THEORY AS A STARTING POINT

The advantages of starting with linguistic theory as a basis for the treatment of philosophical problems are strictly complementary to the previously mentioned disadvantages of the logical empiricist and ordinary language philosophy approaches. First, instead of having to content ourselves with philosophical solutions that rest on the arbitrary principles of some artificial language or on an assortment of comments on the use of certain words or expressions from some natural language, if we base our solutions to philosophical problems on linguistic theory we have a straightforward empirical basis on which to justify such solutions in terms of the empirical evidence that provides the support for successful linguistic descriptions. For the justification of the theoretical constructs used in the solutions is provided by the very same evidence that empirically warrants their introduction into linguistic theory. Hence, we avoid the difficulties that stem from the absence of any empirical controls on a solution to a philosophical problem and from the failure to clarify the relation between facts about the uses of words and expressions and the solutions on behalf of which they are adduced. Second, instead of having to resort to oversimplified and largely unexplained concepts or having no theory at all to appeal to, we can utilize the rich stock of concepts that express the common structure of natural languages, explicitly defined in a formalized theory of linguistic universals, in order to obtain solutions to philosophical problems.

There is a further advantage of this starting point. Basing a solution to a philosophical problem on linguistically universal principles avoids relativizing that solution to one or another particular natural language. Plato and Aristotle wrote in Greek, Descartes in French, Kant in German, and Hume in English. But the philosophical problems about which they wrote were language-independent questions about a common conceptual structure. Accordingly, if it is these problems, rather than some specialized ones having to do exclusively with one language, for which philosophers seek solutions, then we cannot narrow the scope of solutions to philosophical problems. It is just as absurd to say that the solution to a certain philosophical problem is such-and-such in English as it is to say that a broken back is such-and-such a condition among Chinese. By starting with linguistic theory, we can argue from the concepts that underlie language in general to the solution of a philosophical problem, instead of having to argue from concepts that, for all we can say, might underlie only one or another particular language. Furthermore, we can better justify the solution to a philosophical problem because we can adduce far stronger evidence than if we were restricted to the data from one or another particular language (cf. § 3, the concluding remarks of paragraph 3).

5. THE EPISTEMOLOGICAL AND THE PSYCHOLOGICAL

Given that linguistic theory is a formal reconstruction of the universal principles by which speakers relate speech signals and meaningful messages, it is clearly an explication of a facet of a human ability. This makes it in some sense a psychological theory. A philosophical problem, on the other hand, concerns the structure of concepts and the grounds for the validity of cognitive and evaluative principles, which makes it epistemological in the broad sense, not psychological. How, then, can linguistic theory offer solutions to philosophical problems when the 'solutions' are apparently not even addressed to the right type of problem?

This criticism rests on a failure to distinguish two senses of the term 'psychological'. The distinction depends on the difference between a speaker's *linguistic competence*, what he tacitly knows about the structure of his language, and his *linguistic performance*, what he does with this knowledge. A theory in linguistics explicates linguistic competence, not linguistic performance. It seeks to reconstruct the logical structure of the principles that speakers have mastered in attaining fluency. On the other hand, a theory of performance seeks to discover the contribution of each of the factors that interplay to produce natural speech with its various and sundry deviations from ideal linguistic forms. Thus, it must consider such linguistically extraneous factors as memory span, perceptual and motor limitations, lapses of attention, pauses, level of motivation, interest, idiosyncratic and random errors, etc. The linguist, whose aim is to provide a statement of ideal linguistic form unadulterated by the influence of such extraneous factors, can be compared to the logician, whose aim is to provide a statement of ideal implicational form unaldulterated by extraneous factors that influence actual inferences men draw.

Hence, there are two senses of 'psychological': on one, the subject of a psychological theory is a competence, and in the other, a performance. The criticism cited above applies to a proposed solution for a philosophical problem extracted from a theory that is psychological in the latter sense. But it does not apply to one extracted from a theory in linguistics that is psychological in the former. A theory of performance cannot solve a philosophical problem such as that of formulating an inductive logic that is a valid codification of the principles of nondemonstrative inference in science and daily life. People can be quite consistent in drawing nondemonstrative inferences according to invalid principles, and be inconsistent in their practice of using valid ones. Because a theory of performance must accept such behaviour at face value, it has no means of correcting for the acceptance of invalid principles and the rejection of valid ones. In contrast, however, a theory of competence does. Since it regards performance only as evidence for the construction of an idealization, it sifts the facts about behaviour, factoring out the distorting influences of variables that are extraneous to the logical structure of the competence. Such a theory has built in a means for correcting itself in cases where invalid principles were accepted or valid ones rejected. Therefore, linguistic theory cannot be criticized as irrelevant to the solution of philosophical problems.

6. GRAMMATICAL FORM AND LOGICAL FORM

But to establish the relevance of linguistic theory, it must be shown to offer solutions to significant philosophical problems. One of the pervasive problems of modern philosophy is that of distinguishing between the grammatical and logical forms of sentences. It has long been recognized that the phonetic or orthographic realization of many sentences is such that no analysis of them in terms of traditional taxonomic grammar can reveal the true conceptual structure of the proposition(s) that they express. Almost invariably, however, this recognition has led twentieth-century philosophers—Russell, the early Wittgenstein, Carnap, and Ryle, to mention some notable examples—to seek a philosophical theory about the logical form of propositions. They assumed that grammar had done what it could but that its best is not good enough, so that a philosophical theory of one sort or another is needed to exhibit the conceptual relations unmarked in grammatical analysis.

This assumption is open to a serious challenge, even aside from the fact that such philosophical theories have not achieved much success. From the same cases where grammatical form and logical form do not coincide, one can conclude instead that the traditional taxonomic theory of grammar, on which these philosophers' conception of grammatical form is based, is too limited to reveal the underlying conceptual structure of a sentence. Suitably extended, grammar might well reveal the facts about logical form, too. Philosophers who accepted this assumption simply overlooked the possibility that traditional taxonomic grammar might not be the last word on grammar.

The alternative to a philosophical theory about logical form is thus a linguistic theory about logical form. Support for this alternative has come recently from Chomsky's work on syntactic theory which shows that traditional taxonomic grammar is too limited and revises it accordingly.[5] The feasibility of this alternative rests on whether Chomsky's criticism is directed at just the features of traditional taxonomic grammar that make it incapable of handling logical form and on whether the revision provides the theoretical machinery to handle it.

[5] Cf. N. Chomsky, *Syntactic Structures* (Mouton & Co., The Hague, 1957) and P. Postal, *Constituent Structure*, Publication Thirty of the Indiana University Research Centre in Anthropology, Folklore, and Linguistics (Bloomington, 1964).

The traditional taxonomic description of an utterance type is a single labelled bracketing that segments it into continuous phonetic sketches and classifies them as constituents of one, or another sort. Chomsky's basic criticism is that such description cannot mark a variety of syntactic features because it fails to go below the surface structure of sentences. Consider the sentences: (i) 'John is easy to leave' and (ii) 'John is eager to leave'. In a traditional taxonomic description, both receive the same syntactic analysis:

$$((John)_{NP} \ ((is)([\substack{easy \\ eager}])_A \ (to \ leave)_V)_{VP})_S$$

This analysis, which, on the terminology introduced in Section 3, is the superficial phrase-marker for (i) and (ii), does not mark the logical difference that in (i) 'John' is the object of the verb 'leave' whereas in (ii) 'John' is its subject. Consider, further, a sentence like: (iii) 'John knows a kinder person than Bill.' The syntactic ambiguity of (iii) cannot be represented in its taxonomic description because a single (superficial) phrase-marker cannot explicate the different propositional structures underlying the terms of its ambiguity. Finally, consider a normal imperative such as: (iv) 'help him!' Ellipsis, which in such cases absents the subject and future tense auxiliary constituent, cannot be handled by a traditional taxonomic description because it deals only with the phonetically or orthographically realized constituents of a sentence.[6]

These difficulties cannot be remedied by enriching the complexity of superficial phrase-markers. More elaborate segmentation and subclassification cannot overcome the inherent inability of this form of description to represent relational information. Rather, the superficial phrase-marker, as it stands, has a proper role to play in syntactic description, viz. that of providing the most compact representation of the syntactic information required to determine the phonetic shape of a sentence. What is wrong is that the superficial phrase-marker, because it is the only type of description sanctioned by the traditional taxonomic theory of grammar, is made to do work that, in principle, it cannot do so long as it must still play its proper role. To right this wrong, Chomsky introduced the conception of a grammar as a generative, transformational system to supersede the conception of a grammar as a set of segmentation and classification procedures. Within this new conception, Chomsky and others developed the concept of an underlying phrase-marker,[7] a form of syntactic description in which semantically significant grammatical relations can be adequately represented and shown to underlie the phonetic form of sentences on the basis of transformational rules that derive superficial phrase-markers from appropriate underlying phrase-markers by formally specified operations.

---

[6] For the syntactic motivation behind the claim that there are such phonetically unrealized constituents in normal imperatives, cf. P. Postal, 'Underlying and Superficial Linguistic Structures', *The Harvard Educational Review*, XXXIV (1964).

[7] J. J. Katz and P. Postal, op. cit., and N. Chomsky, *Aspects of the Theory of Syntax*. The notion of an underlying phrase-marker used here is the same as Chomsky's notion of a deep phrase-marker.

The logical difference between (i) and (ii) noted above can be indicated with the underlying phrase-markers.[8]

(I) $(((\text{it}) ((\text{one})_{NP} ((\text{leaves})_V (\text{John})_{NP})_{VP})_S)_{NP}((\text{is})(\text{easy}))_{VP})_S$

(II) $((\text{John})_{NP} ((\text{is})((\text{eager})((\text{John})_{NP} (\text{leaves})_{VP})_S)_A)_{VP})_S$

The grammatical relations *subject of* and *object of* are defined in syntactic theory in terms of subconfigurations of symbols in underlying phrase-markers. A simplified version of their definitions is as follows.

Given a configuration of the form $((X)_{NP} (Y)_{VP})_S$ or $((X)_{NP} ((Y)_V (Z)_{NP})_{VP})_S$, *X is the subject of the verb Y and Z is the object of the verb Y.*[9]

By this definition, 'John' in (i) is marked as the object of the verb 'leaves' because it occupies the Z-position and 'leaves' occupies the Y-position in the appropriate subconfiguration of (I), and 'John' in (ii) is marked as the subject of 'leaves' because it occupies the X-position and 'leaves' occupies the Y-position in the appropriate subconfiguration of (II).

Further, since a sentence can be assigned more than one underlying phrase-marker in a transformational syntactic component, syntactic ambiguities like those in (iii) can be represented in terms of appropriately different underlying phrase-markers transformationally associated with the same superficial phrase-marker. Thus, the superficial phrase-marker for (iii), viz.

$((\text{John})_{NP} ((\text{knows})_V ((\text{a})(\text{kinder}) (\text{person})(\text{than})(\text{Bill}))_{NP})_{VP})_S$

is associated with two underlying phrase-markers both of which have the general form,[10]

$((\text{John})_{NP} ((\text{knows})_V ((\text{a})(.\ .\ .)_S(\text{person}))_{NP})_{VP})_S$

but where in one . . . is

$(\text{the person})_{NP}((\text{is})(\text{more})(\text{than})((\text{Bill})_{NP}((\text{is})(\text{kind})_A)_{VP})_S(\text{kind})_A)_{VP}$

while in the other . . . is

$(\text{the person})_{NP}((\text{is})(\text{more})(\text{than})((\text{the})(\text{Bill})_{NP}((\text{knows})_V(\text{the person})_{NP})_{VP})_S (\text{person}))_{NP}((\text{is})(\text{kind})_A)_{VP})_S(\text{kind})_A)_{VP}$

---

[8] For further discussion, cf. G. A. Miller and N. Chomsky, 'Finitary Models of Language Users', *Handbook of Mathematical Psychology*, vol. II, ed. D. R. Luce, R. R. Bush, and E. Galanter (John Wiley & Sons, New York, 1963), pp. 476–80.

[9] Note that this definition reconstructs the intuitive notion that the subject is the noun phrase preceding the verb in a simple sentence and that the object is the noun phrase following it. Restricting the definition to underlying phrase-markers makes it possible to have a single definition because complex sentences are then handled in terms of the simple sentences from which they are constructed.

[10] For further discussion, cf. C. S. Smith, 'A Class of Complex Modifiers in English', *Language*, XXXVII (1961), pp. 342–65.

The former case underlies the term of the ambiguity on which the person that John knows is kinder than Bill is, and the latter case underlies the term on which the person that John knows is kinder than the person Bill knows.

Finally, in ellipsis phonetically unrealized constituents can be specified in underlying phrase-markers and deleted in the transformational derivation of the superficial phrase-marker. This enables us to account for their syntactic relations and their semantic contribution without falsely characterizing the phonetic shape of the sentence, as would be required if we modified the superficial phrase-marker to account for them.

But, although it is clear from these examples that the distinction between underlying and superficial syntactic structure is a significant step toward the philosopher's distinction between logical form and grammatical form, even a fully developed transformational syntactic component would not provide all the theoretical machinery necessary to deal adequately with logical form. Philosophers have rightly held that an analysis of the logical form of a sentence should not only tell us about the formal relations between its constituents, but should also tell us about the semantic properties and relations of the proposition(s) expressed by it. In particular, an account of the logical form of a sentence should specify whether it is (1) *semantically anomalous* (i.e. whether it expresses any proposition at all), (2) *semantically ambiguous* (i.e. whether it expresses more than one proposition, and if so, how many), (3) *a paraphrase of a given sentence* (i.e. whether the two sentences express the same proposition), (4) *analytic*, (5) *contradictory*, (6) *synthetic*, (7) *inconsistent with a given sentence*, (8) *entails* or *is entailed by a given sentence*, (9) *a presupposition of a given sentence*, and so on.

The fact that a transformational syntactic component does not suffice, by itself, to determine such semantic properties and relations has brought about the formulation of a conception of a semantic component designed to determine them.[11] This conception is based on the idea that a speaker's ability to produce and understand sentences he has never before spoken or heard depends on his mastery of principles according to which the meaning of new and unfamiliar sentences can be obtained by a process in which the meaning of syntactically compound constituents is composed out of the meanings of their parts. The semantic component formally reconstructs these compositional principles. It has a *dictionary* that contains an account of the meaning of each syntactically atomic constituent in the language, i.e. representations of the senses of *lexical items*, and a set of *projection rules* that provide the combinatorial machinery for representing the senses of compound constituents on the basis of representations of the senses of the lexical items that make them up. The dictionary

[11] J. J. Katz and J. A. Fodor, 'The Structure of a Semantic Theory', *Language*, XXXIX (1963), pp. 170–210; reprinted in *The Structure of Language: Readings in the Philosophy of Language*, ed. J. A. Fodor and J. J. Katz (Prentice-Hall Inc., Engelwood Cliffs, 1964), pp. 479–518; J. J. Katz, 'Recent Issues in Semantic Theory', *Foundations of Language*, vol. 3, no. 2 (1967), pp. 124–94.

is a list of *entries*, each of which consists of a lexical item written in phonological form, a set of syntactic features, and a set of *lexical readings*. A lexical reading, which represents one sense of a lexical item, consists of a set of *semantic markers* and a *selection restriction*.

A semantic marker is a theoretical term representing a class of equivalent concepts. For example, the semantic marker (Physical Object) represents the class of concepts of a material entity whose parts are spatially and temporally contiguous and move in unison each of us has in mind when we distinguish the meanings of words like 'chair', 'stone', 'man', 'building', etc., from the meanings of words like 'virtue', 'togetherness', 'shadow', 'after-image', etc. Semantic markers enable us to state empirical generalizations about the senses of words (expressions, and sentences), for, by including the semantic marker (Physical Object) in a lexical reading for each of the words in the former group and excluding it from the lexical readings for words in the latter, we thereby express the generalization that the former words are similar in meaning in this respect but that the latter are not. A selection restriction states a condition—framed in terms of a requirement about the presence or absence of certain semantic markers—under which a reading of a constituent can combine with readings of other constituents to form *derived readings* representing conceptually congruous senses of syntactically compound constituents.

The semantic component operates on underlying phrase-markers, converting them into *semantically interpreted underlying phrase-markers*, which formally represent all the information about the meaning of the sentences to which they are assigned. Initially, each of the lexical items in an underlying phrase-marker receives a subset of the lexical readings that it has in its dictionary entry. Then, the projection rules combine lexical readings from sets assigned to different lexical items to form derived readings, and these are combined to form further derived readings, and so on. Each derived reading is assigned to the compound constituent whose parts are the constituents whose readings were combined to form the derived reading. In this way each constituent in the underlying phrase-marker, including the whole sentence, is assigned a set of readings that represents its senses. Thus, a semantically interpreted underlying phrase-marker is an underlying phrase-marker each of whose brackets is assigned a maximal set of readings (where by 'maximal' is meant that the set contains every reading that can be formed by the projection rules without violating a selection restriction).

We are now in a position to define the notions 'logical form' and 'grammatical form': *The logical form of a sentence is the set of its semantically interpreted underlying phrase-markers; the grammatical form of a sentence is its superficial phrase-marker with its phonetic representation.* Accordingly, the syntactic and semantic components for a language comprise a theory of logical form for that language, while the syntactic and phonological components for the language comprise a theory of grammatical form for it. Similarly, syntactic theory and semantic theory comprise a theory of logical form in general, while syntactic theory and phonological theory comprise a theory of grammatical form in general.

7. SEMANTIC PROPERTIES AND RELATIONS

However, semantic theory does much more than complete the account of the distinction between logical form and grammatical form. It also provides solutions to the philosophical problems of explicating concepts such as (1) through (9). Definitions of these concepts thus constitute further support for the relevance of the thesis that I am defending.

Restricting our attention to syntactically unambiguous sentences, we can provide a general idea of such definitions. First, a sentence is semantically anomalous just in case the set of readings assigned to it is empty. This explicates the notion that what prevents a sentence from having a meaningful interpretation are conceptual incongruities between senses of its parts that keep these senses from compositionally forming a sense for the whole sentence. Second, a sentence is semantically unique. i.e. expresses exactly one proposition, just in case the set of readings assigned to it contains one member. Third, a sentence is semantically ambiguous just in case the set of readings assigned to it contains n members, for $n > 1$. Fourth, a sentence is a paraphrase of another sentence just in case the set of readings assigned to them have a member in common. Fifth, two sentences are full paraphrases just in case each is assigned the same set of readings. Sixth, a sentence is analytic if there is a reading assigned to it that is derived from a reading for its subject and a reading for its verb phrase such that the latter contains no semantic markers not already in the former.[12] Finally, a sentence entails another sentence if each semantic marker in the reading for the latter's subject is already contained in the reading for the former's subject and each semantic marker in the reading for the latter's verb phrase is already contained in the reading for the former's verb phrase.[13]

The adequacy of these definitions as solutions to the philosophical problems to which they are addressed is entirely a matter of their empirical justification. Since such definitions are part of a semantic theory, which, in turn, is part of linguistic theory, they must be justified on the same evidential basis as any other linguistic

---

[12] This is a simplified version of the definition of analyticity given in J. J. Katz, 'Analyticity and Contradiction in Natural Language', *The Structure of Language: Readings in the Philosophy of Language*, and in J. J. Katz, *The Philosophy of Language*. This concept of analyticity may be regarded as a linguistically systematized version of Kant's concept of analyticity, with two refinements: one, that Kant's somewhat vague and restricted notions of subject and predicate are replaced by the formally defined grammatical relations *subject of S* and *verb phrase of S*, and two, that Kant's metaphorical notions of concept and of containment are replaced by the formal analogues of a reading and the inclusion of a set of semantic markers in another set. The semantic properties of contradiction and syntheticity can also be defined, as can inconsistency and other related cases; their definitions, however, involve too many technicalities to be given here.

[13] A conditional sentence is analytic just in case its antecedent entails its consequent.

universal. Thus, their empirical evaluation consists in verifying the predictions to which they lead about the semantic properties and relations of sentences from natural languages. Given the semantically interpreted underlying phrase-marker for a sentence S in a language L and the definition of a semantic property P or relation R, we can deduce a prediction about whether S has P or bears R to some other sentence. This deduction is merely a matter of determining whether or not the semantically interpreted underlying phrase-marker(s) of S possess the formal features required by the definition of P or R. Such predictions can be checked against the ways that fluent speakers of L sort sentences in terms of their naive linguistic intuitions. Hence, the justification of these definitions depends on whether such predictions accord with the judgements of fluent speakers about clear cases from L.

To remove from these definitions the stigma that automatically attaches to definitions of semantic properties and relations since Quine's attack on the analytic-synthetic distinction, I will show how the above definition of analyticity avoids the criticism he levelled against Carnap's explication of analyticity.[14] This case is chosen as our example because of its prominence in the literature, but what I am going to say by way of a defence against Quine's criticism of this concept will apply directly to similar criticisms of any of the other semantic properties and relations.

One of Quine's major criticisms was that Carnap's explication of analyticity, contradiction, and related concepts merely defines one of these concepts in terms of others, whose own definition quickly brings us back to the original one without offering a genuine analysis of any of them. The above definition of analyticity, however, cannot be criticized on grounds of such circularity because it is not the case that any of these related terms, or any others for that matter, were used to define it. The unique feature of the above definitions is that the defining condition in each is stated exclusively in terms of a different set of formal features in semantically interpreted underlying phrase-markers. Moreover, no appeal to such definitions is made in the process whereby a semantically interpreted underlying phrase-marker obtains the formal features by virtue of which it satisfies such a defining condition. Further, Quine criticizes Carnap for merely labelling sentences as analytic without ever indicating just what is attributed to a sentence so labelled. On Carnap's account, the term 'analytic' is just an unexplained label. But, on our account, labelling a sentence as analytic depends on its semantic structure, as determined by its semantically interpreted underlying phrase-marker. Thus, labelling a sentence as analytic attributes to it that semantic structure formalized in the definition that introduces 'analytic' into linguistic theory. Lastly, the definition of 'analytic', as well as that of any of the other semantic properties and relations defined in semantic theory, cannot be criticized for being too particularistic because, as Quine requires, they are formulated for variable S and L. This language-independent generality is guaranteed by the

[14] W. V. Quine, 'Two Dogmas of Empiricism', *From a Logical Point of View* (Harvard University Press, Cambridge, 1953).

fact that they are given in linguistic theory and that their defining conditions are formulated exclusively in terms of semantically interpreted underlying phrase-markers, which are associated with each sentence in any linguistic description.[15]

8. SEMANTIC CATEGORIES

The last philosophical problem whose solution I here want to treat within linguistic theory is that of semantic categories, the most general classes into which the concepts from all fields of knowledge divide. The most influential treatment of semantic categories was certainly Aristotle's. Aristotelian categories claim to be the most abstract classificational divisions under which ideas of any sort can be subsumed. They are the ultimate, unanalysable, maximally general set of natural kinds that are given in natural languages. Aristotle enumerated ten (perhaps eight) such categories: *substance*, *quantity*, *quality*, *relation*, *place*, *time*, *posture*, *possession*, *action*, and *passivity* (with the last two of somewhat questionable status). But he did not explain how he chose these categories nor how he decided that no others belong to the list. The criterion he mentions falls short of providing a satisfactory principle for categoryhood.

Aristotle's criterion comes to this: each category is the most general answer to a question of the form 'What is X?'. Thus, *substance* qualifies as a category because 'a substance' is the most general answer to such questions as 'What is Socrates?'. Likewise, *quality* is a category because 'a quality' is the most general answer to such questions as 'What is green?'. There is, of course, much room for doubt about these answers, but, even if this criterion were fairly successful in picking out cases that we would intuitively regard as among the most abstract classificational divisions in our conceptual system, it would tell us nothing about the nature of the categories it sorted out. Its application relies on intuitive judgements about what are and what are not the most general answers to the test questions, without clarifying either for ourselves or our informants just what makes these judgements appropriate judgements about the concepts concerned. Consequently, assuming that those things that are proper answers to such questions are just those things that are the most general genera for classifying concepts, still, we know no more about the idea of a category than we did before having obtained its extension in this manner. The criterion itself presupposes our intuitive understanding of the notion *maximal generality in the domain of possible concepts* as a condition for its application, but it does not provide any analysis of this notion.

If we can embed the theory of semantic categories into linguistic theory, we can obtain an analysis of this notion and thereby arrive at a clearer understanding of

---

[15] For a more detailed and complete account of how my explication of analyticity avoids Quine's criticisms of Carnap's explication, see J. J. Katz, 'Some Remarks on Quine on Analyticity', *The Journal of Philosophy*, vol. LXIV (1967), pp. 36–52.

semantic categories. To do this, we have to ask by what means can we distinguish two sets of semantic markers: *first*, the subset of the set of semantic markers appearing in the dictionary of a linguistic description of some particular language whose members represent concepts having the required degree of generality in that language, and, *second*, the subset of the set of universal semantic markers (as given in semantic theory) whose members represent concepts having the required degree of generality for language in general. Thus, we must provide some empirically motivated way for determining the semantic categories of a particular language and the semantic categories of natural language.

As we have characterized the entries for lexical items in the dictionary of a semantic component, lexical readings contain a semantic marker for each independent conceptual component of the sense that they represent. Formulated in this way, almost every lexical reading would exhibit a high degree of redundancy in the manner in which it specifies the semantic information in a sense. For example, the semantic markers (Physical Object) and (Human) that appear in the lexical readings for the words 'bachelor', 'man', 'spinster', 'child', etc., are subject to a regularity governing their occurrence with respect to one another in the dictionary, viz. whenever (Human) occurs in a lexical reading, so does (Physical Object). Hence, the occurrence of (Physical Object) in lexical readings that contain (Human) is actually redundant, by virtue of the generalization that the occurrence of (Physical Object) is determined by the occurrence of (Human). However, as we have so far described the dictionary, we have made no provision for the formulation of such generalizations. That is, at present, we have no way to express this regularity in the formalism of semantic theory so that the redundancy of (Physical Object) for these cases is forced on us in order that we be able to fully represent the senses of these words. Without a means for expressing such regularities, linguistic descriptions that are written in accord with semantic theory, as so far formulated, can be correctly criticized for having missed an important generalization about their languages. With a means of representing such regularities, the actual occurrence of the semantic marker (Physical Object) is dispensable because its occurrence in the lexical readings for 'bachelor', 'man', 'spinster', etc., is predictable from the occurrence of (Human) in these lexical readings and the generalization that says that (Human) never occurs in a lexical reading unless (Physical Object) occurs. Moreover, this case is not an isolated one. Not only is there a broader regularity covering the occurrence of (Physical Object), viz. whenever (Human), (Animal), (Artifact), (Plant), etc., occurs in a lexical reading, so does (Physical Object), but other semantic markers besides (Physical Object) are redundant in the same way, and are similarly predictable from generalizations expressing the appropriate regularities, viz. (Animal) occurs whenever (Mammal) does. Hence, from the viewpoint of the whole dictionary with its thousands of entries, there will be an incredible amount of redundancy in the specification of the senses of lexical items unless we provide some way to eliminate such unnecessary occurrences of semantic markers by finding some formalism to express these lexical generalizations.

The obvious way to make dictionary entries more economical and to provide a means of expressing these regularities is to extend the conception of the dictionary presented in Section 6 so that the dictionary includes rules which state the appropriate generalizations and thereby enable us to exclude redundant semantic markers from lexical readings. In general, these rules will be of the form

$$(M_1) \lor (M_2) \lor \ldots \lor (M_n) \rightarrow (M_k)$$

where (M_k) is distinct from each (M_i), $1 \leqslant i \leqslant n$ and where $\lor$ is the symbol for disjunction. In the case discussed above, we have an example of a rule of this type.

$(M_1) \lor (M_2) \lor \ldots \lor$ (Human) $\lor$ (Animal) $\lor$ (Artifact) $\lor$ (Plant) $\lor \ldots \lor (M_n) \rightarrow$ (Physical Object)

Adding this rule to the dictionary enables us to capitalize on the regularity noted above and economize lexical readings that contain one of the semantic markers (M_1), (M_2), $\ldots$, (Human), (Animal), (Artifact), (Plant) $\ldots$, (M_n) by dropping the occurrence of the semantic marker (Physical Object) from those lexical readings. Such rules will comprise a new component of the dictionary, whose list of entries can now contain only lexical readings in maximally reduced form. These rules thus function to compress the readings in dictionary entries, making the dictionary a more economical formulation of the lexical information in the language.

So much for the formalism. The redundancy rules not only simplify the statement of the dictionary and state significant lexical generalizations, they also represent inclusion relations among the concepts represented by semantic markers. For such rules can be interpreted as saying that the concepts represented by the semantic markers on the left-hand side of the arrow are included in, or subsumed under, the concept represented by the semantic marker on the right-hand side. Here, then, is where the application of this formalism to the question of semantic categories comes in. Using the redundancy rules in the dictionary of a linguistic description for a language L, we can formally determine which of the semantic markers in that linguistic description represents the semantic categories of L. *We define a semantic category of* L *to be any concept represented by a semantic marker that occurs on the right-hand side of some rule in the redundancy rules in the dictionary of the linguistic description of* L, *but does not occur on the left-hand side of any rule in that set of redundancy rules.* Thus, to find the semantic categories of a particular language, we simply check over the list of redundancy rules in the linguistic description of L and pick each semantic marker for which there is a rule that says that that marker subsumes other markers, and for which there is no rule that says that that marker is subsumed under other markers. The significance of this definition is two-fold. First, it makes it possible for us to formally determine the semantic categories for a given language with respect to a linguistic description for it. Second, it makes it possible to justify empirical claims to the effect that such-and-such concepts are the semantic categories for a given language. Such justification for a set of putative semantic categories is a matter of empirically establishing that no simpler formulation of the lexical readings in the dictionary of the language is provided by redundancy rules other than those which, by the above definition of semantic categories of L, yield the set of putative semantic categories in question. This is the same sort of empirical justification appealed to in other branches of science when it is claimed that some theoretical account is best because it employs the simplest laws for describing the phenomena under study.

On the basis of these considerations, we can also formally determine the semantic markers that represent semantic categories of language in general, i.e. the semantic categories for all natural languages as opposed to the semantic categories of some particular natural language. *We define the semantic categories of language to be those concepts represented by the semantic markers belonging to the intersection of the sets of semantic categories for each particular natural language* $L_1, L_2, \ldots, L_n$, *as obtained from the redundancy rules in the dictionaries of the linguistic descriptions for* $L_1, L_2, \ldots, L_n$ *in the manner just described.* That is, a semantic category of language is a concept represented by a semantic marker that is found in each and every set of semantic categories for particular natural languages. The significance of this definition is parallel to that of the previous one. First, it provides us with a formal means to determine the categories of language, and second, it provides us with a clear-cut empirical basis for deciding what is a semantic category of language. The justification for a claim that some concept is a semantic category of language can be given on the basis of the same evidence that warrants the claims that that concept is a semantic category of $L_1, L_2, \ldots, L_n$.

Notice, finally, that the unexplicated notion of maximal generality on which the Aristotelian notion of categories is based is here explicated formally, in terms of membership in the set of semantic markers that comprises the intersection of the sets of semantic markers that are semantic categories for the natural languages, where each of the semantic markers in these latter sets is obtained by the condition that it appears on the right-hand side of a redundancy rule but not on the left-hand side of any.

9. THE SCOPE OF PHILOSOPHICAL RELEVANCE

If the considerations put forth in this paper on behalf of the thesis that linguistic theory is relevant to the solution of philosophical problems are convincing, then it is quite natural to ask to what philosophical problems is linguistic theory *ir*relevant. That there are problems to which linguistic theory is irrelevant need not be questioned, for the philosophy of mathematics and the philosophy of science provide abundant examples. Consequently, it would be highly desirable to have some handy criterion by which to decide whether a philosophical problem is essentially about the underlying conceptual structure of natural languages or about something else. But I find it hard to believe that we can have such a criterion, for not only do philosophical problems not come to us ear-marked as either linguistic or non-linguistic but, even given a fully developed linguistic theory, it would require considerable further inquiry to discover whether some portion of that theory is relevant to some particular philosophical problem and much further argument to establish that the relevance is such that linguistic theory provides an authentic solution for it.

We have so far considered only one sense in which linguistic theory can be relevant to philosophical questions. In conclusion, I would like to consider another way in which it can have philosophical relevance, one that does not depend on the theory offering us the concepts that answer the philosophical question.

The problem of innate ideas, the crux of the controversy between empiricists and rationalists, is a case to which linguistic theory has a significant application in a somewhat different way than the one in which it applies to the problems discussed above.[16] This problem can be recast as the question of whether the acquisition of a natural language can be explained better on the basis of the empiricist hypothesis that the mind starts out as a *tabula rasa*, or on the basis of the rationalist hypothesis that the mind starts out with a rich stock of innately fixed principles which determine the general form of the rules for a natural language. Given that the child obtains his inner representation of the rules of a language from the linguistic data to which he is exposed during his formative years, we may consider the child's mind to be a black box whose input is such linguistic data and whose output is an internalization of the linguistic description of the language. Accordingly, we ask whether the empiricist hypothesis that this internalization is obtained by processing sensory data on the basis of principles of associative learning, or the rationalist hypothesis that this internalization is obtained by a specialization of the innate system of principles when they are activated by appropriate sensory stimulation, is the better account of how the black box converts its input into its output. We have a fairly clear idea of the associative principles with which the empiricist is willing to credit the child's mind prior to experience, but it is by no means clear what are the innately fixed principles concerning the general form of language on the rationalist's account. Here the relevance of linguistic theory is, then, that it provides a statement of the principles required to formulate the rationalist hypothesis in specific terms. The question is, therefore, whether we must assume as rich a conception of innate structure as is given by linguistic theory's account of the universals of language in order to explain language acquisition.

[16] For a more complete discussion of the problem of innate ideas, cf. Ch. 5 of my book, *The Philosophy of Language*.

Notice, however, that although this question, which reformulates the problem of innate ideas, can only be raised in an explicit form when linguistic theory supplies the conception of innate structure for the rationalist hypothesis, its answer is not given by linguistic theory. Linguistic theory does not validate the rationalist position in its controversy with the empiricist position, since it is outside the scope of linguistic theory to decide which of these two positions is best supported by the facts about the linguistic information available to the child and about how he copes with them.

This case was introduced not only to show that the relevance of linguistic theory to philosophy goes beyond solving philosophical problems, but also to show that it can be relevant in the specific sense of providing the means by which a philosophical problem can be reformulated in a manner that makes it more susceptible to solution. Whether linguistic theory is relevant to philosophical investigation in still other ways must remain a matter for further philosophical and linguistic inquiry.

VII

SYMPOSIUM ON INNATE IDEAS

(a) RECENT CONTRIBUTIONS
TO THE THEORY OF INNATE IDEAS
Summary of Oral Presentation

NOAM CHOMSKY

I THINK that it will be useful to separate two issues in the discussion of our present topic—one is the issue of historical interpretation, namely, what in fact was the content of the classical doctrine of innate ideas, let us say, in Descartes and Leibniz; the second is the substantive issue, namely, in the light of the information presently available, what can we say about the prerequisites for the acquisition of knowledge —what can we postulate regarding the psychologically *a priori* principles that determine the character of learning and the nature of what is acquired.

These are independent issues; each is interesting in its own right, and I will have a few things to say about each. What I would like to suggest is that contemporary research supports a theory of psychological *a priori* principles that bears a striking resemblance to the classical doctrine of innate ideas. The separateness of these issues must, nevertheless, be kept clearly in mind.

The particular aspect of the substantive issue that I will be concerned with is the problem of acquisition of language. I think that a consideration of the nature of linguistic structure can shed some light on certain classical questions concerning the origin of ideas.

To provide a framework for the discussion, let us consider the problem of designing a model of language-acquisition, an abstract 'language-acquisition device' that duplicates certain aspects of the achievement of the human who succeeds in acquiring linguistic competence. We can take this device to be an input-output system

$$\text{data} \rightarrow \boxed{\text{LA}} \rightarrow \text{knowledge}$$

To study the substantive issue, we first attempt to determine the nature of the output in many cases, and then to determine the character of the function relating input

From *Boston Studies in the Philosophy of Science*, vol. III (The Humanities Press, New York, 1968), pp. 81–107. Reprinted by permission of the authors, New York: Humanities Press Inc., and D. Reidel Publishing Company.

to output. Notice that this is an entirely empirical matter; there is no place for any dogmatic or arbitrary assumptions about the intrinsic, innate structure of the device LA. The problem is quite analogous to the problem of studying the innate principles that make it possible for a bird to acquire the knowledge that expresses itself in nest-building or in song-production. On *a priori* grounds, there is no way to determine the extent to which an instinctual component enters into these acts. To study this question, we would try to determine from the behaviour of the mature animal just what is the nature of its competence, and we would then try to construct a second-order hypothesis as to the innate principles that provide this competence on the basis of presented data. We might deepen the investigation by manipulating input conditions, thus extending the information bearing on this input-output relation. Similarly, in the case of language-acquisition, we can carry out the analogous study of language-acquisition under a variety of different input conditions, for example, with data drawn from a variety of languages.

In either case, once we have developed some insight into the nature of the resulting competence, we can turn to the investigation of the innate mental functions that provide for the acquisition of this competence. Notice that the conditions of the problem provide an upper bound and a lower bound on the structure that we may suppose to be innate to the acquisition device. The upper bound is provided by the diversity of resulting competence—in our case, the diversity of languages. We cannot impose so much structure on the device that acquisition of some attested language is ruled out. Thus we cannot suppose that the specific rules of English are innate to the device and these alone, since this would be inconsistent with the observation that Chinese can be learned as readily as English. On the other hand, we must attribute to the device a sufficiently rich structure so that the output can be attained within the observed limits of time, data, and access.

To repeat, there is no reason for any dogmatic assumptions about the nature of LA. The only conditions we must meet in developing such a model of innate mental capacity are those provided by the diversity of language, and by the necessity to provide empirically attested competence within the observed empirical conditions.

When we face the problem of developing such a model in a serious way, it becomes immediately apparent that it is no easy matter to formulate a hypothesis about innate structure that is rich enough to meet the condition of empirical adequacy. The competence of an adult, or even a young child, is such that we must attribute to him a knowledge of language that extends far beyond anything that he has learned. Compared with the number of sentences that a child can produce or interpret with ease, the number of seconds in a lifetime is ridiculously small. Hence the data available as input are only a minute sample of the linguistic material that has been thoroughly mastered, as indicated by actual performance. Furthermore, great diversity of input conditions does not lead to a wide diversity in resulting competence, so far as we can detect. Furthermore, vast differences in intelligence have only a small effect on resulting competence. We observe further that the tremendous intellectual accomplishment of language-acquisition is carried out at a period of life when the child is capable of little else, and that this task is entirely beyond the capacities of an otherwise intelligent ape. Such observations as these lead one to suspect, from the start, that we are dealing with a species-specific capacity with a largely innate component. It seems to me that this initial expectation is strongly supported by a deeper study of linguistic competence. There are several aspects of normal linguistic competence that are crucial to this discussion.

I. CREATIVE ASPECT OF LANGUAGE USE

By this phrase I refer to the ability to produce and interpret new sentences in independence from 'stimulus control'—i.e. external stimuli or independently identifiable internal states. The normal use of language is 'creative' in this sense, as was widely noted in traditional rationalist linguistic theory. The sentences used in everyday discourse are not 'familiar sentences' or 'generalizations of familiar sentences' in terms of any known process of generalization. In fact, even to speak of 'familiar sentences' is an absurdity. The idea that sentences or sentence-forms are learned by association or conditioning or 'training', as proposed in recent behaviourist speculations, is entirely at variance with obvious fact. More generally, it is important to realize that in no technical sense of these words can language use be regarded as a matter of 'habit' or can language be regarded as 'a complex of dispositions to respond'.

A person's competence can be represented by a *grammar*, which is a system of rules for pairing semantic and phonetic interpretations. Evidently, these rules operate over an infinite range. Once a person has mastered the rules (unconsciously, of course), he is capable, in principle, of using them to assign semantic interpretations to signals quite independently of whether he has been exposed to them or their parts, as long as they consist of elementary units that he knows and are composed by the rules he has internalized. The central problem in designing a language acquisition device is to show how such a system of rules can emerge, given the data to which the child is exposed. In order to gain some insight into this question, one naturally turns to a deeper investigation of the nature of grammars. I think real progress has been made in recent years in our understanding of the nature of grammatical rules and the manner in which they function to assign semantic interpretations to phonetically represented signals, and that it is precisely in this area that one can find results that have some bearing on the nature of a language-acquisition device.

II. ABSTRACTNESS OF PRINCIPLES OF SENTENCE INTERPRETATION

A grammar consists of syntactic rules that generate certain underlying abstract objects, and rules of semantic and phonological interpretation that assign an intrinsic meaning and an ideal phonetic representation to these abstract objects.

Concretely, consider the sentence 'The doctor examined John'. The phonetic form of this sentence depends on the intrinsic phonological character of its minimal items ('The', 'doctor', 'examine', 'past tense', 'John'), the bracketing of the sentence (that is, as $\big[\,[[the]\ [doctor]]\ [[examined]\ [John]]\,\big]$), and the categories to which the bracketed elements belong (that is, the categories 'Sentence', 'Noun-Phrase', 'Verb', 'Noun', 'Determiner', in this case). We can define the 'surface structure' of an utterance as its labelled bracketing, where the brackets are assigned appropriate categorial labels from a fixed, universal set. It is transparent that grammatical relations (e.g. 'Subject-of', 'Object-of', etc.) can be defined in terms of such a labelled bracketing. With terms defined in this way, we can assert that there is very strong evidence that the phonetic form of a sentence is determined by its labelled bracketing by phonological rules that operate in accordance with certain very abstract but quite universal principles of ordering and organization.

The meaning of the sentence 'the doctor examined John' is, evidently, determined from the meanings of its minimal items by certain general rules that make use of the grammatical relations expressed by the labelled bracketing. Let us define the 'deep structure' of a sentence to be that labelled bracketing that determines its intrinsic meaning, by application of these rules of semantic interpretation. In the example just given, we would not be far wrong if we took the deep structure to be identical with the surface structure. But it is obvious that these cannot in general be identified. Thus consider the slightly more complex sentences: 'John was examined by the doctor'; 'someone persuaded the doctor to examine John'; 'the doctor was persuaded to examine John'; 'John was persuaded to be examined by the doctor'. Evidently, the grammatical relations among *doctor, examine,* and *John,* as expressed by the deep structure, must be the same in all of these examples as the relations in 'the doctor examined John'. But the surface structures will differ greatly.

Furthermore, consider the two sentences:

> someone expected the doctor to examine John
> someone persuaded the doctor to examine John.

It is clear, in this case, that the similarity of surface structure masks a significant difference in deep structure, as we can see, immediately, by replacing 'the doctor to examine John' by 'John to be examined by the doctor' in the two cases.

So far, I have only made a negative point, namely, that deep structure is distinct from surface structure. Much more important is the fact that there is very strong evidence for a particular solution to the problem of how deep and surface structures are related, and how deep and surface structures are formed by the syntactic component of the grammar. The details of this theory need not concern us for the present. A crucial feature of it, and one which seems inescapable, is that it involves formal manipulations of structures that are highly abstract, in the sense that their relation to signals is defined by a long sequence of formal rules, and that, consequently, they have nothing remotely like a point by point correspondence to signals. Thus sentences may have very similar underlying structures despite the great diversity of physical form, and diverse underlying structures despite similarity of surface form. A theory of language acquisition must explain how this knowledge of abstract underlying forms and the principles that manipulate them comes to be acquired and freely used.

III. UNIVERSAL CHARACTER OF LINGUISTIC STRUCTURE

So far as evidence is available, it seems that very heavy conditions on the form of grammar are universal. Deep structures seem to be very similar from language to language, and the rules that manipulate and interpret them also seem to be drawn from a very narrow class of conceivable formal operations. There is no *a priori* necessity for a language to be organized in this highly specific and most peculiar way. There is no sense of 'simplicity' in which this design for language can be intelligibly described as 'most simple'. Nor is there any content to the claim that this design is somehow 'logical'. Furthermore, it would be quite impossible to argue that this structure is simply an accidental consequence of 'common descent'. Quite apart from questions of historical accuracy, it is enough to point out that this structure must be rediscovered by each child who learns the language. The problem is, precisely, to determine how the child determines that the structure of his language has the specific characteristics that empirical investigation of language leads us to postulate, given the meagre evidence available to him. Notice, incidentally, that the evidence is not only meagre in scope, but very degenerate in quality. Thus the child learns the principles of sentence formation and sentence interpretation on the basis of a corpus of data that consists, in large measure, of sentences that deviate in form from the idealized structures defined by the grammar that he develops.

Let us now return to the problem of designing a language-acquisition device. The available evidence shows that the output of this device is a system of recursive rules that provide the basis for the creative aspect of language use and that manipulate highly abstract structures. Furthermore, the underlying abstract structures and the rules that apply to them have highly restricted properties that seem to be uniform over languages and over different individuals speaking the same language, and that seem to be largely invariant with respect to intelligence and specific experience. An engineer faced with the problem of designing a device meeting the given input-output conditions would naturally conclude that the basic properties of the output are a consequence of the design of the device. Nor is there any plausible alternative to this assumption, so far as I can see. More specifically, we are led by such evidence as I have mentioned to suppose that this device in some manner incorporates: a phonetic theory that defines the class of possible phonetic representations; a semantic theory that defines the class of possible semantic representations; a schema that defines the class of possible grammars; a general method for interpreting grammars that assigns a semantic and phonetic interpretation to each sentence, given a grammar; a method of evaluation that assigns some measure of 'complexity' to grammars.

Given such a specification, the device might proceed to acquire knowledge of a language in the following way: the given schema for grammar specifies the class of possible hypotheses; the method of interpretation permits each hypothesis to be tested against the input data; the evaluation measure selects the highest valued grammar compatible with the data. Once a hypothesis—a particular grammar—is selected, the learner knows the language defined by this grammar; in particular, he is capable of pairing semantic and phonetic interpretations over an indefinite range of sentences to which he has never been exposed. Thus his knowledge extends far beyond his experience and is not a 'generalization' from his experience in any significant sense of 'generalization' (except, trivially, the sense defined by the intrinsic structure of the language-acquisition device).

Proceeding in this way, one can seek a hypothesis concerning language-acquisition that falls between the upper and lower bounds, discussed above, that are set by the nature of the problem. Evidently, for language learning to take place the class of possible hypotheses—the schema for grammar—must be heavily restricted.

This account is schematic and idealized. We can give it content by specifying the language-acquisition system along the lines just outlined. I think that very plausible and concrete specifications can be given, along these lines, but this is not the place to pursue this matter, which has been elaborately discussed in many publications on transformational generative grammar.

I have so far been discussing only the substantive issue of the prerequisites for acquisition of knowledge of language, the *a priori* principles that determine how and in what form such knowledge is acquired. Let me now try to place this discussion in its historical context.

First, I mentioned three crucial aspects of linguistic competence: (1) creative aspect of language use; (2) abstract nature of deep structure; (3) apparent universality of the extremely special system of mechanisms formalized now as transformational grammar. It is interesting to observe that these three aspects of language are discussed in the rationalist philosophy of the 17th century and its aftermath, and that the linguistic theories that were developed within the framework of this discussion are, in essence, theories of transformational grammar.

Consequently, it would be historically accurate to describe the views regarding language structure just outlined as a rationalist conception of the nature of language. Furthermore, I employed it, again, in the classical fashion, to support what might fairly be called a rationalist conception of acquisition of knowledge, if we take the essence of this view to be that the general character of knowledge, the categories in which it is expressed or internally represented, and the basic principles that underlie it, are determined by the nature of the mind. In our case, the schematism assigned as an innate property to the language-acquisition device determines the form of knowledge (in one of the many traditional senses of 'form'). The role of experience is only to cause the innate schematism to be activated, and then to be differentiated and specified in a particular manner.

In sharp contrast to the rationalist view, we have the classical empiricist assumption that what is innate is (1) certain elementary mechanisms of peripheral processing (a receptor system), and (2) certain analytical mechanisms or inductive principles or mechanisms of association. What is assumed is that a preliminary analysis of experience is provided by the peripheral processing mechanisms and that one's concepts and knowledge, beyond this, are acquired by application of the innate inductive principles to this initially analysed experience. Thus only the procedures and mechanisms for acquisition of knowledge consititute an innate property. In the case of language-acquisition, there has been much empiricist speculation about what these mechanisms may be, but the only relatively clear attempt to work out some specific account of them is in modern structural linguistics, which has attempted to elaborate a system of inductive analytic procedures of segmentation and classification that can be applied to data to determine a grammar. It is conceivable that these methods might be somehow refined to the point where they can provide the surface structures of many utterances. It is quite inconceivable that they can be developed to the point where they can provide deep structures or the abstract principles that generate deep structures and relate them to surface structures. This is not a matter of further refinement, but of an entirely different approach to the question. Similarly, it is difficult to imagine how the vague suggestions about conditioning and associative nets that one finds in philosophical and psychological speculations of an empiricist cast might be refined or elaborated so as to provide for attested competence. A system of rules for generating deep structures and relating them to surface structures, in the manner characteristic of natural language, simply does not have the properties of an associative net or a habit family; hence no elaboration of principles for developing such structures can be appropriate to the problem of designing a language-acquisition device.

I have said nothing explicit so far about the doctrine that there are innate ideas and innate principles of various kinds that determine the character of what can be known in what may be a rather restricted and highly organized way. In the traditional view a condition for these innate mechanisms to become activated is that appropriate stimulation must be presented. This stimulation provides the occasion for the mind to apply certain innate interpretive principles, certain concepts that proceed from 'the power of understanding' itself, from the faculty of thinking rather than from external objects. To take a typical example from Descartes (Reply to Objections, V): '. . . When first in infancy we see a triangular figure depicted on paper, this figure cannot show us how a real triangle ought to be conceived, in the way in which geometricians consider it, because the true triangle is contained in this figure, just as the statue of Mercury is contained in a rough block of wood. But because we already possess within us the idea of a true triangle, and it can be more easily conceived by our mind than the more complex figure of the triangle drawn on paper, we, therefore, when we see the composite figure, apprehend not it itself, but rather the authentic triangle' (Haldane and Ross, vol. II, p. 227). In this sense, the idea of triangle is innate. For Leibniz what is innate is certain principles (in general, unconscious), that 'enter into our thoughts, of which they form the soul and the connection'. 'Ideas and truths are for us innate as inclinations, dispositions, habits, or natural potentialities.' Experience serves to elicit, not to form, these innate structures. Similar views are elaborated at length in rationalist speculative psychology.

It seems to me that the conclusions regarding the nature of language-acquisition, discussed above, are fully in accord with the doctrine of innate ideas, so understood, and can be regarded as providing a kind of substantiation and further development of this doctrine. Of course, such a proposal raises non-trivial questions of historical interpretation.

What does seem to me fairly clear is that the present situation with regard to the study of language learning, and other aspects of human intellectual achievement of comparable intricacy, is essentially this. We have a certain amount of evidence about the grammars that must be the output of an acquisition model. This evidence shows clearly that knowledge of language cannot arise by application of step-by-step inductive operations (segmentation, classification, substitution procedures, 'analogy', association, conditioning, and so on) of any sort that have been developed or discussed within linguistics, psychology, or philosophy. Further empiricist speculations contribute nothing that even faintly suggests a way of overcoming the intrinsic limitations of the methods that have so far been proposed and elaborated. Furthermore, there are no other grounds for pursuing these empiricist speculations, and avoiding what would be the normal assumption, unprejudiced by doctrine, that one would formulate if confronted with empirical evidence of the sort sketched above. There is, in particular, nothing known in psychology or physiology that suggests that the empiricist approach is well motivated, or that gives any grounds for scepticism concerning the rationalist alternative sketched above.

For further discussion of the question of historical interpretation, see Chomsky, *Aspects of the Theory of Syntax* (1965), Ch. 1, and *Cartesian Linguistics* (1966). For further discussion of matters touched on here, see also Chomsky, 'Explanatory Models in Linguistics', in *Logic, Methodology and Philosophy of Science*, ed. by

E. Nagel, P. Suppes, and A. Tarski (1962); J. Katz, *The Philosophy of Language* (1966); P. M. Postal, Review of A. Martinet, *Elements of General Linguistics* (1966); and the selections in section VI of *The Structure of Language, Readings in the Philosophy of Language*, ed. by J. Fodor and J. Katz (1964).

(b) THE 'INNATENESS HYPOTHESIS' AND EXPLANATORY MODELS IN LINGUISTICS

HILARY PUTNAM

I. THE INNATENESS HYPOTHESIS

THE 'innateness hypothesis' (henceforth, the 'I.H.') is a daring—or apparently daring; it may be meaningless, in which case it is not daring—hypothesis proposed by Noam Chomsky. I owe a debt of gratitude to Chomsky for having repeatedly exposed me to the I.H.; I have relied heavily in what follows on oral communications from him; and I beg his pardon in advance if I misstate the I.H. in any detail, or misrepresent any of the arguments for it. In addition to relying upon oral communications from Chomsky, I have also relied upon Chomsky's paper 'Explanatory Models in Linguistics', in which the I.H. plays a considerable role.

To begin, then, the I.H. is the hypothesis that the human brain is 'programmed' at birth in some quite *specific* and *structured* aspects of human natural language. The details of this programming are spelled out in some detail in 'Explanatory Models in Linguistics'. We should assume that the speaker has 'built in'[1] a function which assigns weights to the grammars G_1, G_2, G_3, . . . in a certain class Σ of transformational grammars. Σ is not class of all *possible* transformational grammars; rather all the members of Σ have some quite strong similarities. These similarities appear as 'linguistic universals'—i.e. as characteristics of *all* human natural languages. If intelligent non-terrestrial life—say, Martians—exists, and if the 'Martians' speak a language whose grammar does not belong to the subclass Σ of the class of all transformational grammars, then, I have heard Chomsky maintain, humans (except possibly for a few geniuses or linguistic experts) would be unable to learn Martian; a human child brought up by Martians would fail to acquire language; and Martians would, conversely, experience similar difficulties with human tongues. (Possible

---

[1] What 'built in' means is highly unclear in this context. The weighting function by itself determines only the relative ease with which various grammars can be learned by a human being. If a grammar G_1 can be learned more easily than a grammar G_2, then doubtless this is 'innate' in the sense of being a fact about human learning *potential*, as opposed to a fact about what has been learned. But this sort of fact is what learning theory tries to account for; *not* the explanation being sought. It should be noticed that Chomsky has never offered even a schematic account of the sort of device that is supposed to be present in the brain, and that is supposed to do the job of selecting the highest weighted grammar compatible with the data. But only a description, or at least a theory, of such a device could properly be called an innateness *hypothesis* at all.

difficulties in *pronunciation* are not at issue here, and may be assumed *not* to exist for the purposes of this argument.) As examples of the similarities that all grammars of the subclass Σ are thought to possess (above the level of phonetics), we may mention the *active–passive* distinction, the existence of a *non-phrase-structure* portion of the grammar, the presence of such major categories as *concrete noun*, *verb taking an abstract subject*, etc. The project of delimiting the class Σ may also be described as the project of defining a *normal form for grammars*. Conversely, according to Chomsky, any non-trivial normal form for grammars, such that correct and perspicuous grammars of all human languages can and should be written in that normal form, 'constitutes, in effect, a hypothesis concerning the innate intellectual equipment of the child'.[2]

Given such a highly *restricted* class Σ of grammars (highly restricted in the sense that grammars not in the class are perfectly conceivable, not more 'complicated' in any absolute sense than grammars in the class, and may well be employed by non-human speakers, if such there be), the performance of the human child in learning his native language may be understood as follows, according to Chomsky. He may be thought of as operating on the following 'inputs'[3]: a list of utterances, containing both grammatical and ungrammatical sentences; a list of corrections, which enable him to classify the input utterances *as* grammatical or ungrammatical; and some information concerning which utterances count as *repetitions* of earlier utterances. Simplifying slightly, we may say that, on this model, the child is supplied with a list of grammatical sentence *types* and a list of ungrammatical sentence *types*. He then 'selects' the grammar in Σ compatible with this information to which his weighting function assigns the highest weight. On this scheme, the general *form* of grammar is not learned from experience, but is 'innate', and the 'plausibility ordering' of grammars compatible with given data of the kinds mentioned is likewise 'innate'.

So much for a statement of the I.H. If I have left the I.H. vague at many points, I believe that this is no accident—for the I.H. seems to me to be *essentially* and *irreparably* vague—but this much of a statement may serve to indicate *what* belief it is that I stigmatize as irreparably vague.

A couple of remarks may suffice to give some idea of the role that I.H. is supposed to play in linguistics. Linguistics relies heavily, according to Chomsky, upon 'intuitions' of grammaticality. But *what* is an intuition of 'grammaticality' an intuition *of*? According to Chomsky, the sort of theory-construction programmatically outlined above is what is needed to give this question the only answer it can have or deserves to have. Presumably, then, to 'intuit' (or assert, or conjecture, etc.) that a sentence is grammatical is to 'intuit' (or assert, or conjecture, etc.) that the sentence is generated by the highest-valued G_i in the class Σ which is such that it generates

---

[2] 'Explanatory Models in Linguistics', p. 550.
[3] 'E. M. in L.', pp. 530–531.

all the grammatical sentence types with which we have been supplied by the 'input' and none of the ungrammatical sentence types listed in the 'input'.[4]

Chomsky also says that the G_i which receives the highest value must do *more* than agree with 'intuitions' of grammaticality; it must account for certain ambiguities, for example.[5] At the same time, unfortunately, he lists no semantical information in the input, and he conjectures[6] that a child needs semantical information only to 'provide motivation for language learning', and not to arrive at the *formal* grammar of its language. Apparently, then, the fact that a grammar which agrees with a sufficient amount of 'input' must be in the class Σ to be 'selected' by the child is what rules out grammars that generate all and only the grammatical sentences of a given natural language, but fail to correctly 'predict'[7] ambiguities (cf. 'E. M. in L.', p. 533).

In addition to making clear what it *is* to be grammatical, Chomsky believes that the I.H. confronts the linguist with the following tasks: To *define* the normal form for grammars described above, and to *define* the weighting function. In *Syntactic Structures* Chomsky, indeed, gives this as an objective for linguistic theory: to give an *effective* procedure for choosing between rival grammars.

Lastly, the I.H. is supposed to justify the claim that what the linguist provides is 'a hypothesis about the innate intellectual equipment that a child brings to bear in language learning'.[8] Of course, even if language is *wholly* learned, it is still true that linguistics 'characterizes the linguistic abilities of the mature speaker',[9] and that a grammar 'could properly be called an explanatory model of the linguistic intuition of the native speaker'.[10] However, one could with equal truth say that a driver's manual 'characterizes the car-driving abilities of the mature driver' and that a calculus text provides 'an explanatory model of the calculus-intuitions of the mathematician'. Clearly, it is the idea that *these* abilities and *these* intuitions are close to the human *essence*, so to speak, that gives linguistics its 'sex appeal', for Chomsky at least.

---

[4] I doubt that the child really is told which sentences it hears or utters are *ungrammatical*. At most it is told which are *deviant*—but it may not be told which are deviant for *syntactical* and which for *semantical* reasons.

[5] Many of these—e.g. the alleged 'ambiguity' in 'the shooting of the elephants was heard'—*require coaching to detect*. The claim that grammar 'explains the ability to recognize ambiguities' thus lacks the impressiveness that Chomsky believes it to have. I am grateful to Paul Ziff and Stephen Leeds for calling this point to my attention.

[6] 'E. M. in L', p. 531, n. 5.

[7] A grammar 'predicts' an ambiguity, in Chomsky's formalism, whenever it assigns two or more structural descriptions to the same sentence.

[8] 'E. M. in L.', p. 530.

[9] 'E. M. in L.', p. 530.

[10] 'E. M. in L.', p. 533.

II. THE SUPPOSED EVIDENCE FOR THE I.H.

A number of empirical facts and alleged empirical facts have been advanced to support the I.H. Since limitations of space make it impossible to describe all of them here, a few examples will have to suffice.

(a) the *ease* of the child's original language learning. 'A young child is able to gain perfect mastery of a language with incomparably greater ease [*than an adult*—H. P.] and without any explicit instruction. Mere exposure to the language, and for a remarkably short period, seems to be all that the normal child requires to develop the competence of the native speaker.'[11]

(b) The fact that reinforcement, 'in any interesting sense', seems to be unnecessary for language learning. Some children have apparently even learned to speak without *talking*,[12] and then displayed this ability at a relatively late age to startled adults who had given them up for mutes.

(c) The ability to 'develop the competence of the native speaker' has been said not to depend on the intelligence level. Even quite low I.Q.'s 'internalize' the grammar of their native language.

(d) The 'linguistic universals' mentioned in the previous section are allegedly accounted for by the I.H.

(e) Lastly, of course, there is the 'argument' that runs '*what else* could account for language learning?' The task is so incredibly complex (analogous to learning, at least implicitly, a complicated physical theory, it is said), that it would be miraculous if even one tenth of the human race accomplished it without 'innate' assistance. (This is like Marx's 'proof' of the Labour Theory of Value in *Capital*, vol. III, which runs, in essence, '*What else* could account for the fact that commodities have different value *except* the fact that the labour-content is different?')

III. CRITICISM OF THE ALLEGED EVIDENCE

A. The Irrelevance of Linguistic Universals

1. Not surprising on any theory

Let us consider just how surprising the 'linguistic universals' cited above really are. Let us assume for the purpose a community of Martians whose 'innate intellectual equipment' may be supposed to be as different from the human as is compatible with their being able to speak a language at all. What could we expect to find in their language?

If the Martians' brains are not vastly richer than ours in complexity, then they,

---

[11] 'E. M. in L.', p. 529.
[12] Macaulay's *first* words, it is said, were: 'Thank you, Madam, the agony has somewhat abated' (to a lady who had spilled hot tea on him).

like us, will find it possible to employ a practically infinite set of expressions only if those expressions possess a 'grammar'—i.e. if they are built up by recursive rules from a limited stock of basic forms. Those basic forms need not be built up out of a *short* list of phonemes—the Martians might have vastly greater memory capacity than we do—but if Martians, like humans, find rote learning difficult, it will not be surprising if they too have *short* lists of phonemes in their languages.

Are the foregoing reflections arguments *for* or *against* the I.H.? I find it difficult to tell. If belief in 'innate intellectual equipment' is *just* that, then how *could* the I.H. be false? How could something with *no* innate intellectual equipment *learn* anything? *To be sure*, human 'innate intellectual equipment' is relevant to language learning; if this means that such parameters as memory span and memory capacity play a crucial role. But what rank Behaviourist is supposed to have ever denied *this*? On the other hand, that a particular mighty arbitrary set Σ of grammars is 'built in' to the brain of *both* Martians and Humans is *not* a hypothesis we would have to invoke to account for *these* basic similarities.

But for what similarities above the level of phonetics, where constitutional factors play a large role for obvious reasons, *would* the I.H. have to be invoked *save* in the trivial sense that memory capacity, intelligence, needs, interests, etc., are all relevant to language learning, and all depend in part, on the biological make-up of the organism? If Martians are such strange creatures that they have no interest in physical objects, for example, their language will contain no concrete nouns; but would not this be *more*, not *less* surprising, on any *reasonable* view, than their having an interest in physical objects? (Would it be surprising if Martian contained devices for forming truth-functions and for quantification?)

Two more detailed points are relevant here. Chomsky has pointed out that no natural language has a phrase-structure grammar. But this too is not surprising. The sentence 'John and Jim came home quickly' is not generated by a phrase-structure rule, in Chomsky's formalization of English grammar. But the sentence 'John came home quickly and Jim came home quickly' *is* generated by a phrase-structure rule in the grammar of mathematical logic, and Chomsky's famous 'and-transformation' is just an abbreviation rule. Again, the sentence 'That was the lady I saw you with last night' is not generated by a phrase-structure rule in English, or at least not in Chomsky's description of English. But the sentence 'That is $\iota\chi$ (χ is a lady and I saw you with χ last night)' is generated by a phrase-structure rule in the grammar of mathematical logic. And again the idiomatic English sentence *can* be obtained from its phrase-structure counterpart by a simple rule of abbreviation. Is it really surprising, does it really point to anything more interesting than *general intelligence*, that these operations which break the bounds of phrase-structure grammar appear in every natural language?[13]

---

[13] Another example of a transformation is the 'active-passive' transformation (cf. *Syntactic Structures*). But (a) the presence of this, if it *is* a part of the grammar, is not surprising—why should not there be a

Again, it may appear startling at first blush that such categories as noun, verb, adverb, etc., have 'universal' application. But, as Curry has pointed out, it is too easy to multiply 'facts' here. If a language contains nouns—that is, a phrase-structure category which contains the proper names—it contains noun phrases, that is, phrases which occupy the environments of nouns. If it contains noun phrases it contains verb phrases—phrases which when combined with a noun phrase by a suitable construction yield sentences. If it contains verb phrases, it contains adverb phrases— phrases which when combined with a verb phrase yield a verb phrase. Similarly, adjective phrases, etc., can be defined in terms of the *two* basic categories 'noun' and 'sentence'. Thus the existence of nouns is all that has to be explained. And this reduces to explaining two facts: (1) The fact that all natural languages have a large phrase-structure portion in their grammar, in the sense just illustrated, in spite of the effect of what Chomsky calls 'transformations'. (2) The fact that all natural languages contain proper names. But (1) is not surprising in view of the fact that phrase-structure rules are extremely simple algorithms. Perhaps Chomsky would reply that 'simplicity' is subjective here, but this is just not so. The fact is that all the natural measures of complexity of an algorithm—size of the machine table, length of computations, time, and space required for the computation—lead to the same result here, quite independently of the detailed structure of the computing machine employed. Is it surprising that algorithms which are 'simplest' for virtually any computing system we can conceive of are also simplest for naturally evolved 'computing systems'? And (2)—the fact that all natural languages contain proper names —is not surprising in view of the utility of such names, and the difficulty of always finding a definite description which will suffice instead.

Once again, 'innate' factors are relevant *to be sure*—if choosing *simple* algorithms as the basis of the grammar is 'innate', and if the need for identifying persons rests on something innate—but what Behaviourist would or should be surprised? Human brains are computing systems and subject to some of the constraints that affect all computing systems; human beings have a natural interest in one another. If *that* is 'innateness', well and good!

---

systematic way of expressing the *converse* of a relation?—and (b) the argument for the existence of such a 'transformation' at all is extremely slim. It is contended that a grammar which 'defines' active and passive forms separately (this can be done by even a phrase-structure grammar) fails to represent something that every speaker knows, viz. that active and passive forms are *related*. But why must every *relation* be mirrored by *syntax*? Every 'speaker' of the canonical languages of mathematical logic is aware that each sentence (χ) $(F\chi \supset G\chi)$ is related to a sentence (χ) $(\overline{G}\chi \supset \overline{F}\chi)$; yet the definition of 'well formed formula' fails to mirror 'what every speaker knows' in this respect, and is not inadequate on that account.

2. Linguistic universals could be accounted for, even if surprising, without invoking the I.H.

Suppose that language-using human beings evolved *independently* in two or more places. Then, if Chomsky were *right*, there should be two or more *types* of human beings descended from the two or more original populations, and normal children of each type should fail to learn the languages spoken by the other types. Since we do not observe this, since there is only *one* class Σ built into *all* human brains, we have to conclude (if the I.H. is true) that language-using is an evolutionary 'leap' that occurred only *once*. But in that case, it is overwhelmingly likely that all human languages are descended from a single original language, and that the existence today of what are called 'unrelated' languages is accounted for by the great lapse of time and by countless historical changes. This is, indeed, likely even if the I.H. is false, since the human race itself is now generally believed to have resulted from a single evolutionary 'leap', and since the human population was extremely small and concentrated for millennia, and only gradually spread from Asia to other continents. Thus, even if language-using was learned or invented rather than 'built in', or even if only some general dispositions in the direction of language using are 'built in',[14] it is likely that some one group of humans first developed language as we know it, and then spread this through conquest or imitation to the rest of the human population. Indeed, we do know that this is just how *alphabetic* writing spread. In any case, I repeat, this hypothesis—a single origin for human language—is certainly *required* by the I.H., but much weaker than the I.H.

But just this *consequence* of the I.H. is, in fact, enough to account for 'linguistic universals'! For, if all human languages are descended from a common parent, then just such highly useful features of the common parent as the presence of some kind of quantifiers, proper names, nouns, and verbs, etc., would be expected to survive. Random variation may, indeed, alter many things; but that it should fail to strip language of proper names, or common nouns, or quantifiers, is not so surprising as to require the I.H.

B. The 'Ease' of Language Learning is not Clear

Let us consider somewhat closely the 'ease' with which children do learn their native language. A typical 'mature' college student seriously studying a foreign language spends three hours a week in lectures. In fourteen weeks of term he is thus exposed to forty-two hours of the language. In four years he may pick up over 300 hours of the language, very little of which is actual listening to native informants. By contrast, direct-method teachers estimate that 300 hours of direct-method teaching will enable

[14] It is very difficult to account for such phenomena as the spontaneous babbling of infants without *this* much 'innateness'. But this is not to say that a class Σ and a function f are 'built in', as required by the I.H.

one to converse fluently in a foreign language. Certainly 600 hours—say, 300 hours of direct-method teaching and 300 hours of reading—will enable any adult to speak and read a foreign language with ease, and to use an incomparably larger vocabulary than a young child.

It will be objected that the adult does not acquire a perfect accent. So what? The adult has been speaking one way all of his life, and has a huge set of habits to unlearn. What can equally well be accounted for by learning theory should not be cited as evidence for the I.H.

Now the child by the time it is four or five years old has been exposed to *vastly* more than 600 hours of direct method instruction. Moreover even if 'reinforcement' is not necessary, most children are consciously and repeatedly reinforced by adults in a host of ways—e.g. the constant repetition of simple one-word sentences ('cup', 'doggie') in the presence of babies. Indeed, any foreign adult living with the child for those years would have an incomparably better grasp of the language than the child does. The child indeed has a better accent. Also, the child's grammatical mistakes, which are numerous, arise not from carrying over previous language habits, but from not having fully acquired the first set. But it seems to me that this 'evidence' for the I.H. stands the facts on their head.

C. Reinforcement another Issue

As Chomsky is aware, the evidence is today slim that *any* learning requires reinforcement 'in any interesting sense'. Capablanca, for example, learned to play chess by simply watching adults play. This is comparable to Macaulay's achievement in learning language without speaking. Non-geniuses normally do require practice both to speak correctly and to play chess. Yet probably anyone *could* learn to speak *or* to play chess without practice if muffled, in the first case, or not allowed to play, in the second case, with sufficiently prolonged observation.

D. Independence of Intelligence Level an Artifact

Every child learns to speak the native language. What does this mean? If it means that children do not make serious grammatical blunders, even by the standards of descriptive as opposed to prescriptive grammar, this is just not true for the young child. By nine or ten years of age this has ceased to happen, perhaps (I speak as a parent), but nine or ten years is enough time to become pretty darn good at *anything*. What is more serious is what 'grammar' *means* here. It does not include mastery of vocabulary, in which even many adults are deficient, nor ability to understand *complex* constructions, in which many adults are *also* deficient. It means purely and simply the ability to learn what every *normal* adult learns. Every normal adult learns what every adult learns. What this 'argument' reduces to is 'Wow! How complicated a skill every normal adult learns. What else could it be but *innate*.' Like the preceding argument, it reduces to the 'What Else' argument.

But what of the 'What Else?' argument? Just how impressed should we be by the failure of current learning theories to account for complex learning processes such as those involved in the learning of language? If Innateness were a *general* solution, perhaps we should be impressed. But the I.H. *cannot*, by its very nature, *be* generalized to handle all complex learning processes. Consider the following puzzle (called 'jump'):

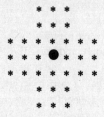

To begin with, all the holes but the centre one are filled. The object of the game is to remove all the pegs but one by 'jumping' (as in checkers) and to end with the one remaining peg in the centre. A clever person can get the solution in perhaps eight or ten hours of experimentation. A not so clever person can get a 'near-solution'—two pegs left—in the same time. No programme exists, to my knowledge, that would enable a computer to solve even the 'near solution' problem without running out of both time and space, even though the machine can spend the equivalent of many human lifetimes in experimentation. When we come to the discovery of even the simplest mathematical theorem the situation is even more striking. The theorems of mathematics, the solutions to puzzles, etc., cannot on *any* theory be *individually* 'innate'; what must be 'innate' are heuristics, i.e. learning strategies. In the absence of any knowledge of what *general multipurpose learning strategies* might even look like, the assertion that such strategies (which absolutely must exist and be employed by all humans) cannot account for this or that learning process, that the answer or an answer schema must be 'innate', is utterly unfounded.

I will be told, of course, that *everyone* learns his native language (as well as everyone does), and that not everyone solves puzzles or proves theorems. But everyone does learn pattern recognition, automobile driving, etc., and everyone in fact can solve many problems that no computer can solve. In conversation Chomsky has repeatedly used precisely such skills as these to support the idea that humans have an 'innate conceptual space'. Well and good, if true. *But that is no help. Let a complete seventeenth-century Oxford University education be innate if you like*; still the solution to 'jump' was not innate; the Prime Number Theorem was not innate;

and so on. *Invoking 'Innateness' only postpones the problem of learning; it does not solve it.* Until we understand the strategies which make general learning possible—and vague talk of 'classes of hypotheses' and 'weighting functions' is utterly useless here—no discussion of the *limits* of learning can even begin.

(c) THE EPISTEMOLOGICAL ARGUMENT

NELSON GOODMAN

(Jason has brought back from the nomads of Outer Cantabridgia something that Anticus suspects is more fleece than golden.)

ANTICUS: Tell me about the resurrection.

JASON: After some centuries, the theory of Innate Ideas has been disinterred, and enthroned as the only adequate explanation for some striking facts concerning human linguistic proficiency.

A: What facts?

J: In the first place, that all natural languages, however diverse in origin and in superficials, have certain remarkable properties in common.

A: But is it remarkable that the elements of any collection have some remarkable properties in common? Surely we can find throughout the random deals of a pack of cards during an evening some very special uniformities; but we do not take them as posing a problem.

J: The claim is of course much stronger: that any language a human being can acquire has the properties in question.

A: I can imagine having a good deal of trouble mastering a language with an alphabet of a million letters and no word less than a million letters long. But does this call for elaborate explanation?

J: The properties in question are more interesting properties of grammatical form and of meaning.

A: Then the claim is indeed material and testable. I suppose these nomads have constructed languages lacking the properties in question, and found that earnest efforts to teach them to human beings fail. This seems to me not only remarkable but incredible; for the human mind strikes me as agile enough to learn, with appropriate instruction and explanation, almost any transformation or distortion of an already familiar language.

J: I have done them an injustice. They hold only that no language lacking the properties in question can be acquired by a human being as an *initial* language. Once one language is available and can be used for giving explanation and instruction, the limitations are transcended.

A: That answers my objection; but now I am puzzled as to how they propose to examine the claim experimentally. Can they really take an infant at birth, isolate it from all the influences of our language-bound culture, and attempt to inculcate it with one of the 'bad' artificial languages?

J: No. They readily admit this cannot be done. They regard their claim as a hypothesis not subject to such direct experimental test, but supported by ancillary considerations and evidence.

A: Very well; the claim is that certain statements about the properties of languages that can be initially acquired are plausible, and a certain explanation illuminating. But so far we have been speaking vaguely of 'certain properties' or 'the properties in question'. If we are to judge plausibility, we must surely have a clearer formulation or illustrations of what these properties are.

J: My informants are not always very explicit about this. They cite some general grammatical properties now and then; but I know you would say that each of these has been tailored to fit the known natural languages and derives rather from the conceptual apparatus we impose upon these languages than from any remarkable affinities among them. One case that might carry some weight with you, though, concerns a concocted language called *Grubleen*. It differs from ordinary English only in that it contains the predicates 'grue' (for 'examined before *t* and green or not so examined and blue') and 'bleen' (for 'examined before *t* and blue or not so examined and green') instead of the predicates 'green' and 'blue'. The claim is that while a user of ordinary English might be taught to use *Grubleen*, no human being could acquire Grubleen as an initial language.

A: Though, as you say, experimental support for this can hardly be expected. But I have another worry. Let us assume that we now have before us an example of a language that cannot be so acquired. Still, what in general is the difference between Grubleen-like and English-like languages? I see by your gesture that you are painfully aware of the difficulties of answering that question. So far we seem to have concluded first that the claim we are discussing cannot be experimentally tested even when we have an acknowledged example of a 'bad' language, and second that the claim has not even been formulated to the extent of citation of a single general property of 'bad' languages.

J: Nevertheless, important conjectures often cannot in the early stages be either precisely stated or actually tested. What you have said does not convince me that the claim ought to be rejected. If it is suggestive or promising enough, we ought rather to help examine and develop it.

A: You are right in principle; but I am not moved to try in this case, since the claim seems to me discredited by antecedent considerations.

J: Such as?

A: What we call a language is a fairly elaborate and sophisticated symbolic system. Don't you think, Jason, that before anyone acquires a language, he has had an abundance of practice in developing and using rudimentary prelinguistic symbolic systems in which gestures and sensory and perceptual occurrences of all sorts function as signs?

J: Yes; but *language*-acquisition is what is at issue.

A: You remember, though, that the real issue is over *initial* acquisition of languages, since once some language is available, acquisition of others is relatively easy.

J: True; but surely you do not call those rudimentary systems languages.

A: No; but I submit that our facility in going from one symbolic system to another is not much affected by whether each or either or neither is called a language; that acquisition of an initial language is acquisition of a secondary symbolic system; and that as we find no interesting limitations upon what we can acquire as a secondary language, we have no ground for believing that there are such limitations upon what we can acquire as a secondary symbolic system. In other words, when initial-language acquisition is seen as secondary-symbolic-system acquisition, the claim that there are rigid limitations upon initial-language acquisition is deprived of plausibility by the fact that there are no such limitations upon secondary-language acquisition.

J: I am afraid that what you say undermines also a second claim; that initial-language acquisition is astonishingly fast.

A: Yes. If the language were the first symbolic system acquired, and the process of acquisition considered to begin with the first overt use of words, I suppose we might manage to work up some astonishment. But if acquisition of the first language is merely passage from a symbolic system already acquired to another that we are taught, that is a much easier step. On the other hand, if the process of acquiring the first language is thought of as beginning with the first use of symbols, then it must begin virtually at birth and takes a long time.

J: Does not all this just move the question back from the nature of languages that can be initially acquired to the nature of symbolic systems that can be so acquired? I suspect we would find remarkable uniformities and astonishing speed of acquisition here.

A: We'd certainly have an even harder time doing it. Little of the unimpressive evidence adduced with respect to languages would be pertinent here; and obviously we cannot argue back from uniformity of language to uniformity of prelinguistic system. We'd have to examine symbols that are not overt and articulate but rather inaccessible and ill-defined. And since the prelinguistic systems are likely to be fragmentary as well as rudimentary, we'd have trouble deciding when a system is acquired. And experimentation under all these difficulties would have to begin with symbol-using from the moment of birth. But I hardly have to refute your suspicions. Rather than facts crying for a theory, the theory is crying for the facts.

J: Your objections are more telling against my inadequate presentation than against the spirit and substance of what I am trying to present. All sophistry aside, is there nothing in human behaviour you find striking enough to demand special explanation?

A: I can think of some remarkable behavioural facts that call for no such explanation as a theory of innate ideas.

J: For example?

A: Well, I learned instantly to fall when dropped, and moreover to fall, no matter where dropped, precisely toward the centre of the earth.

J: And for this remarkable fact we do need a theory—the theory of gravitation.

A: A set of laws subsuming this behaviour under a very general description; but I am not inclined to attribute knowledge of these laws to the falling objects.

J: But this is mechanical behaviour, common to animate and inanimate objects alike. Living things obey more special laws framed in terms of other notions. And human beings, in their cognitive behaviour, obey still more special laws that require reference to innate ideas.

A: Your speed there is remarkable enough. Let us take it more slowly. Are you saying that human cognition is explicable only by supposing that the mind is supplied at the start with the interpretation of certain symbols? If that means only that it responds in a fixed way to certain stimuli, this suggests a view of mind we would both reject. What seems to me notable is not the fixity but rather the flexibility of the mind; its ability to adapt, adjust, transform; its way of achieving unity in variety, constancy amid instability, of inventing rather than obeying. The mind does not merely kick when tapped; it gropes. The groping and grasping, the seeking and finding, seem to me more characteristic than any mere programme-reading.

J: You Berkeleyans always overstress the groping.

A: And you Leibnizians overstress the predetermination.

J: We go from pettifogging analysis to loose metaphor, and now name-calling! But seriously, I think it is just those capacities of the mind that you praise that can be accounted for only by the instrumentation of innate ideas.

A: We have been paying much less attention to what the theory is than to what it is supposed to explain. Let us now assume that for certain remarkable facts I have no alternative explanation. Of course, that alone does not dictate acceptance of whatever theory may be offered; for that theory might be worse than none. Inability to explain a fact does not condemn me to accept an intrinsically repugnant and incomprehensible theory. Now I gather that the theory here proposed is that certain ideas are implanted in the mind as original equipment.

J: Roughly that.

A: And being ideas, they are in consciousness?

J: No, not necessarily; not even usually.

A: Then they are in the subconscious mind, operating upon cognitive processes, and capable of being brought into full consciousness?

J: Not even that. I may have no direct access to them at all. My only way of discovering them in my own mind may be by the same methods that someone else might use to infer that I have them, or I to infer that he does.

A: Then I am puzzled. You seem to be saying that these innate ideas are neither innate nor ideas.

J: What is innate are not concepts, images, formulae, or pictures, but rather 'inclinations, dispositions, habits, or natural potentialities'.

A: But I thought the ideas were posited to explain the capacities. If all that is claimed is that the mind has certain inclinations and capacities, how can you justify calling these ideas?

J: The justification is historical. Descartes and Leibniz used the term 'innate idea' in just this sense. But after all, it is the theory that counts, not the term 'innate idea'.

A: In that case, why all the effort at historical justification? And why, after admitting the term is controversial and claiming it is unnecessary, do these people go on using it? For a very compelling, but not very good, reason: that until the term 'innate idea' is applied, what is advocated is the rather trivial truth that the mind has certain capacities, tendencies, limitations. Once we apply the term, in anything like its normal use, the thesis becomes far from obvious; but unfortunately, it becomes false or meaningless. John Locke made all this acutely clear.

J: Again I am afraid I have not been careful enough. Rather than identify the innate ideas with capacities, etc., I probably should have said that these ideas exist as or are '*innate as*' such capacities.

A: A few minutes ago you accused me of sophistry; but I bow before the subtlety of that last statement. Go again, Jason, and bring back to me all the mysteries of ideas being innate as capacities. Then, if you like, we can talk again about unsubstantiated conjectures that cry for explanation by implausible and untestable hypotheses that hypostatize ideas that are innate in the mind as non-ideas.

NOTES ON THE CONTRIBUTORS

J. L. AUSTIN was White's Professor of Moral Philosophy at Oxford from 1953 until his early death in 1960. His *Philosophical Papers* were published in 1961, *Sense and Sensibilia* in 1962, and *How To Do Things with Words* also in 1962. The last-named is a version, not fully completed by Austin, of his William James Lectures at Harvard in 1955.

P. F. STRAWSON is Waynflete Professor of Metaphysical Philosophy at Oxford. Among his publications are *An Introduction to Logical Theory* (1952), *Individuals* (1959), and *The Bounds of Sense* (1966). He is the editor of *Philosophical Logic* in the present series.

J. R. SEARLE (the editor of the present volume) is a member of the Department of Philosophy of the University of California at Berkeley. He has contributed many valuable articles to philosophical periodicals, and his book *Speech Acts* was published in 1969.

H. P. GRICE, formerly a Fellow of St. John's College, Oxford, is now a member of the Department of Philosophy at Berkeley. He was William James Lecturer at Harvard in 1966.

NOAM CHOMSKY, of the Massachusetts Institute of Technology, is perhaps the most influential of contemporary writers on linguistic theory. Among his publications are *Syntactic Structures* (1957), *Current Issues in Linguistic Theory* (1964), *Aspects of the Theory of Syntax* (1965), and *Cartesian Linguistics* (1966). He was John Locke Lecturer in Oxford in 1969.

JERROLD J. KATZ, of the Massachusetts Institute of Technology, is the author of *The Problem of Induction and its Solution* (1962), *The Philosophy of Language* (1966), and of many articles. He edited, with J. A. Fodor, *The Structure of Language* (1964).

HILARY PUTNAM, of the Department of Philosophy, Harvard University, has written many valuable papers on the philosophy of science and mathematics, as well as on linguistic theory. He edited, with Paul Benacerraf, *Philosophy of Mathematics: Selected Readings* (1964).

NELSON GOODMAN, of Brandeis University, was John Locke Lecturer in Oxford in 1962. Besides many important papers, he is the author of *The Structure of Appearance* (1951), *Fact, Fiction, and Forecast* (1955), and *Languages of Art* (1968).

BIBLIOGRAPHY

(not including material in this volume)

I. BOOKS

(1) *Modern classics in the philosphy of language*

FREGE, G.: *Philosophical writings*, trans. P. T. Geach and M. Black (Blackwell, Oxford, 1952).

RUSSELL, B.: *Lectures on the philosophy of logical atomism*, reprinted in Russell, *Logic and knowledge*, ed. R. C. Marsh (Allen & Unwin, London, 1956).

WITTGENSTEIN, L.: *Tractatus logico-philosophicus*, trans. D. F. Pears and B. F. McGuinness (Routledge & Kegan Paul, London, 1961).
Philosophical investigations (Blackwell, Oxford, 1953).

(2) *Some recent books*

ALSTON, W.: *The philosophy of language* (Prentice Hall, New Jersey, 1964).

AUSTIN, J. L.: *How to do things with words* (Clarendon Press, Oxford, 1962).

CHOMSKY, N.: *Aspects of the theory of syntax* (M.I.T. Press, Cambridge, Mass., 1965).

GEACH, P. T.: *Reference and generality* (Cornell University Press, Ithaca, 1962).

KATZ, J. J.: *The philosophy of language* (Harper & Row, New York, 1966).

QUINE, W. V. O.: *Word and object* (Technology Press and John Wiley & Son, New York and London, 1960).

RUSSELL, B.: *An inquiry into meaning and truth* (Allen & Unwin, London, 1948).

SEARLE, J. R.: *Speech acts* (Cambridge University Press, London and New York, 1969).

STRAWSON, P. F.: *Individuals* (Methuen, London, 1959).

ZIFF, P.: *Semantic analysis* (Cornell University Press, Ithaca, 1960).

II. ARTICLES ON SELECTED TOPICS

(1) *Reference and the theory of descriptions*

DONELLAN, K. S.: 'Reference and definite descriptions', *Philosophical review* (1966).

FREGE, G.: 'Sense and reference', *Philosophical writings*, trans. P. T. Geach and M. Black (Blackwell, Oxford, 1962).

RUSSELL, B.: 'On Denoting', *Mind* (1905), reprinted *Readings in philosophical analysis*, ed. H. Feigl and W. Sellars (Appleton-Century-Crofts Inc., New York, 1949).
'Mr. Strawson on referring', *Mind* (1957).

STRAWSON, P. F.: 'On referring', *Mind* (1950), reprinted *Essays in conceptual analysis*, ed. A. G. N. Flew (Macmillan, London, 1956).
'Identifying reference and truth values', *Theoria* (1964).

(2) *Speech acts and propositions*

ALSTON, W.: 'Linguistic acts', *American philosophical quarterly* (1965).

AUSTIN, J. L.: 'Performative utterances', *Philosophical papers* (Clarendon Press, Oxford, 1961).

CARTWRIGHT, R.: 'Propositions', *Analytical philosophy*, ed. R. J. Butler (Blackwell, Oxford, 1962).

COHEN, L. J.: 'Do illocutionary forces exist?', *Philosophical quarterly* (1964).

GEACH, P.: 'Assertion', *Philosophical review* (1965).

LEMMON, E. J.: 'Sentences, statements and propositions', *British analytical philosophy*, ed. B. A. O. Williams and A. C. Montefiore (Routledge & Kegan Paul, London, 1966).

SEARLE, J. R.: 'Austin on locutionary and illocutionary acts', *Philosophical review* (1968).

TEICHMAN, J.: 'Propositions', *Philosophical review* (1961).

(3) Meaning

CAVELL, S.: 'Must we mean what we say?', *Inquiry* (1958), reprinted *Ordinary language*, ed. V. Chappell (Prentice Hall, Englewood Cliffs, N.J., 1964).

DAVIDSON, D.: 'Truth and meaning', *Synthèse* (1967).

GRICE, H. P.: 'Meaning', *Philosophical review* (1957), reprinted *Philosophical logic*, ed. P. F. Strawson (Oxford University Press, London, 1967).

RYLE, G.: 'The theory of meaning', *British philosophy in mid-century*, ed. C. A. Mace (Macmillan, New York, 1957).

SHWAYDER, D.: 'Uses of language and uses of words', *Theoria* (1960), reprinted *The theory of meaning*, ed. G. H. R. Parkinson (Oxford University Press, London, 1968).

STAMPE, D. W.: 'Toward a grammar of meaning', *Philosophical review* (1968).

(4) Truth

AUSTIN, J. L.: 'Truth', *Proceedings of the Aristotelian Society*, Supp. vol. (1950), reprinted *Truth*, ed. G. W. Pitcher (Prentice Hall, Englewood Cliffs, N. J., 1964).

DUMMETT, M.: 'Truth', *Proceedings of the Aristotelian Society* (1958–9), reprinted *Philosophical logic*, ed. P. F. Strawson (Oxford University Press, London, 1967).

STRAWSON, P. F.: 'Truth', *Proceedings of the Aristotelian Society*, Supp. vol. (1950), reprinted in *Truth*, ed. G. W. Pitcher (Prentice Hall, Englewood Cliffs, N.J., 1964). 'Truth: a reconsideration of Austin's views', *Philosophical quarterly* (1965).

TARSKI, A.: 'The semantic conception of truth', *Philosophy and phenomelogical research* (1944), reprinted H. Feigl and W. Sellars, *Readings in philosophical analysis* (Appleton-Century-Crofts Inc., New York, 1949).

(5) Philosophical aspects of generative grammar

BOYD, J. and THORNE, J. P.: 'The semantics of modal verbs', *Journal of linguistic studies*, 1969.

CHOMSKY, N.: 'Current issues in linguistic theory', *The structure of language*, ed. J. J. Katz and J. A. Fodor (Prentice Hall, Englewood Cliffs, N.J., 1964).

HARMAN, G.: 'Psychological aspects of the theory of syntax', *The journal of philosophy* (1967).

KATZ, J. J.: 'Analyticity and contradiction in natural languages', *The structure of language*, ed. J. J. Katz and J. A. Fodor (Prentice Hall, Englewood Cliffs, N.J., 1964).

KIPARSKY, P. and KIPARSKY, C.: 'Fact', *Recent advances in Linguistics*, eds. Bierwisch and Heidolph (Mouton, The Hague, 1969).

(6) Analytic propositions

BENNETT, J.: 'Analytic-synthetic', *Proceedings of the Aristotelian Society* (1958–9).

PUTNAM, H.: 'The analytic and the synthetic', *Minnesota studies in the philosophy of science*, vol. III (University of Minn. Press, Minneapolis, 1962).

QUINE, W. V. O.; 'Two dogmas of empiricism', *From a logical point of view* (Harvard University Press, Cambridge, Mass., 1953).

STRAWSON, P. F.: 'Propositions, concepts, and logical truth', *Philosophical quarterly* (1957).

STRAWSON, P. F. and GRICE, H. P.: 'In defense of a dogma', *Philosophical review* (1956).

(7) *Miscellaneous*

BLACK, M.: 'Metaphor', *Models and metaphors* (Cornell University Press, New York, 1961).

GEACH, P. T.: 'Subject and predicate', *Mind* (1950).

TOULMIN, S. and BAIER, K.: 'On describing', *Mind* (1952).

INDEX OF NAMES

(not including authors mentioned only in the Bibliography)